The
Accidental
Leader

The
Accidental
Leader

*What to Do When You're
Suddenly in Charge*

Harvey Robbins
Michael Finley

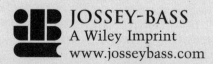

JOSSEY-BASS
A Wiley Imprint
www.josseybass.com

Published by Jossey-Bass
A Wiley Imprint
989 Market Street, San Francisco, CA 94103-1741   www.josseybass.com

Jossey-Bass books and products are available through most bookstores. To contact Jossey-Bass directly call our Customer Care Department within the U.S. at 800-956-7739, outside the U.S. at 317-572-3986, or fax 317-572-4002.

Jossey-Bass also publishes its books in a variety of electronic formats. Some content that appears in print may not be available in electronic books.

Text design by Paula Goldstein.

Library of Congress Cataloging-in-Publication Data

Robbins, Harvey.
    The accidental leader : what to do when you're suddenly in charge / Harvey Robbins, Michael Finley. 1st ed.
        p. cm.
Includes bibliographical references and index.
    ISBN 0-7879-6855-2 (alk. paper)
    1. Leadership. I. Finley, Michael, 1950– II. Title.
    HD57.7.R625 2004
    658.4'092 dc21

                                                    2003011690

Printed in the United States of America
FIRST EDITION
PB Printing   10 9 8 7 6 5 4 3 2 1

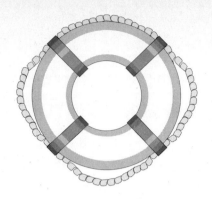

Contents

For our families, gratefully

Who gets called to accidental leadership?
Just about anyone.

- A worker who dropped an idea in the suggestion box, and it was good enough that management took note.
- A teacher who'd never been in charge of anything, but had to take a rotation as department chair.
- A parent volunteer on a school committee who was asked to take a bigger responsibility.
- A team member other team members looked up to.
- A techie who impressed everyone as understanding the business process better than they did.
- A good performer in a sales position who was rewarded by a promotion to sales *supervisor*.
- An administrative executive assistant whose knowledge and intelligence impressed everyone and who wound up standing in for the boss.
- The team leaders whose company downsized its high-paid middle managers and had to find more affordable people to replace them.
- The nearest warm body whose current manager was hired away, and *someone* needed to step in right now.

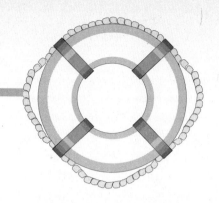

Introduction

What's an Accidental Leader?

You're in a movie, or a dream. You're a junior member of an airline flight crew. Your usual job is serving drinks and giving safety instructions. But something just happened in the cockpit: the pilot and copilot have come down with food poisoning and are puking their guts out in the lavatories.

Someone has to land the plane, and 120 people in coach—mostly nuns, Boy Scouts, and football players—are all looking to *you*.

Your heart is pounding like a kettledrum as you make your way toward the front cabin and sit down at that galaxy of controls. You've got a good attitude, though. You tell yourself, "I can do it, I can do it! I can—"

Then the plane goes into a nosedive.

That's when you wake up, and you are so, so grateful it was a dream. Because statistics say that, despite what you see in the movies, *no flight attendant has ever landed a plane safely.*

It would be nice to think that people elevated to sudden positions of responsibility routinely succeed. But they don't. **Planes are hard to land**. And being put in charge of one—being given a seat in the cockpit—is nothing like knowing how to fly.

Here's an example not involving a jumbo jet in a tailspin:

Fran was the most junior member of Shell Oil's tax and financing department in the 1970s when the department head went down with a massive heart attack. Confusion reigned. No one could decide who should replace him.

"I was the only woman in a group of guys who had been doing this forever," she told the *New York Times* (Jan. 20, 2002). "I decided to devise a plan and called everyone together. My first shock was that they all showed up. Then they all started coming to me for advice."

Before Fran knew it, she was in charge—by accident.

"It was exhilarating, but at the same time it was very scary. I had bit off something and didn't know if I could swallow it."

During one reorganization, she had to lay off 25 percent of the division's workforce. At one facility, she had to tell people to their faces they would all lose their jobs. "When I left the plant and went to the airport bathroom, I threw up."

For Fran, the story worked out well. Thirty years later, she is president and CEO of Shell Chemical LP. She had the native smarts and toughness to survive dozens of crises and challenges to her leadership. But for thousands of new accidental leaders, the outcome is less agreeable.

All over the world, right at this moment, people are getting tapped on the shoulder. They're being told that, starting now, they're going to be in charge of something—a team, a project, an office, a committee, a business unit.

Tag. You're it.

It happens. Existing bosses die, move away, get fired, or are abducted by aliens. Some subordinate is asked to step up and take a stab at being boss. Welcome to accidental leadership.

It happens everywhere, in any size of group, on the for-profit business side or not-for-profit side of community service.

The truth is, accidental leaders are more the rule in this era of disruption and transformation than the non-accidental, corn-fed, MBA-prepared leaders of a very short time ago. And it is the situation of every worker who ever makes the transition from "doing a job" to "being in charge."

Now, getting the tag can be exhilarating—a pathway to greater satisfaction, career development, and personal growth. Many people take to it like fish to water. For a few it's a snap because they have a mentor to guide them through the difficult first days.

For most accidental leaders, however, it's a mess. It means:

- *Minimal training:* Most organizations don't train for leadership.
- *Zero mentoring:* There is a global shortage of great people who will show others how to be competent out of the kindness of their hearts.
- *Sink-or-swim desperation:* If you get tagged and screw up, that's the last tag you'll ever get.
- *And time's a-wasting:* You can figure you have a hundred or so days to get it together before the people who are so fond of you now lose confidence.

Let's be honest about this: **Most accidental leaders have a pretty rocky time of it.** Many of them freak out, change their styles all around, try desperately to hide their managerial weaknesses, and generally come across as nervous, not-ready-for-prime-time wrecks. The costs of this rockiness are huge:

- Lost time for the company or project, which translates to missed opportunities
- Bewildered colleagues who wonder why you don't just tell them *what to do*
- And toasted careers for the leaders who couldn't lead (because when they fail, they don't usually slink back to their earlier positions—they're often through with the organization *forever*)

It's tough, going from Joe or Jo Schmo to Big Boss overnight. Accidental leaders face a gauntlet of seemingly irreconcilable challenges:

- How do you demonstrate to your higher-ups that you're up to this challenge . . . at the same time you demonstrate to your "lower-downs" that leadership hasn't gone to your head?

- How do you achieve the existing goals for the superiors that promoted you ("Good dog!") . . . at the same time you engender an entrepreneur's spirit of daring?
- How do you fill people with hope to achieve great things . . . knowing there is the distinct possibility you may have to fire them some day?
- How do you simultaneously maintain the status quo as a proficient manager . . . while as a leader you share your vision of a better way to do things?

These are the dark fears that afflict the accidental leader. And unless they are dealt with and replaced with sensible action, the accidental leader is merely an interim leader—until the next person gets tagged.

So it looks like you're on your own. Only you can save your career. One false move, and you're not just gone from the new position, you part company with the organization forever. Because that's how it works.

Well, take heart. The book in your hands right now (unless you are holding it with your feet) is a handbook for people thrust into positions of sudden responsibility. You'll see that it's not long on theory or long-term options. It's about **what to do now**, in the moment of panicky transformation. We're going to explain to you:

- How to get over the shock of getting tagged
- How to figure out what you bring to the challenge—your pluses and minuses
- How to define success, and how to achieve it
- How to get other people on your side, or in any event not against you

- How to overcome your natural shortcomings
- How to get organized, if you've never been organized before
- How to see through the apparent system to the culture within
- How to tell people stuff, and get them to act on it
- How to breathe when the general culture is rancid
- How to keep the people you lead from driving you crazy
- How to turn failure into success, and how to celebrate when you're done
- How to do all these things without wearing yourself to a frazzle

Think of this book as emergency equipment. Keep it close to you, like a life vest, because it has the answers to questions that will be making you crazy.

We can't guarantee twenty years of career longevity, but we'll keep you afloat till you figure out what to do next.

The
Accidental
Leader

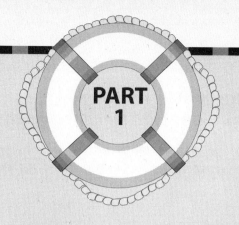

Managing
Oneself

Three ways to cope with leader's anxiety:

1. **Give yourself time to sort things out**. Of course you're in a whirl the first day. Don't expect to behave like Yoda when you feel more like Luke Skywalker.
2. **Self-talk**. Answer back when you berate yourself. No, maybe you're not a Harvard MBA, but you've been around the block a few times. Don't puff yourself up unrealistically, but don't deflate yourself, either. Remind yourself, "This isn't about *me*. It's about the *mission,* and all I have to do is move people toward it."
3. **Point yourself toward success**. Envision a positive future, then take the appropriate steps to get you there.

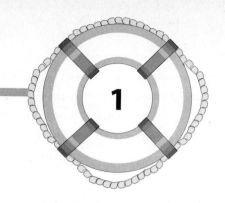

Coming to Terms with Responsibility

I couldn't believe how I acted," said Beverly, who was promoted from clerk to third shift supervisor at a Denver check clearinghouse. "I got the news. I went home. I scarfed down a half-gallon of butter pecan ice cream."

Or Joshua, tagged to become assistant manager at a Bangor, Maine, convenience store: "I freaked. I'm still a student. I like having a job where I can just go through the motions. As soon as they told me, my mind started flashing the word *failure.*"

Bev and Josh flipped out when they got the call to become leaders. To them it immediately represented frightening change. It's like their personalities rebelled against the notion of leadership:

- "I've never led anything in my life."
- "Great, now everyone will know how incompetent I am."
- "What funny papers have these people been reading?"

Is panic useful or good in any way? **Not in this situation**. When we lived in caves and a saber-toothed tiger wandered in the door, it was useful to experience an adrenaline rush. It shut down other systems—thinking, for instance—and narrowed our options to two, each highly demanding of our bodies, fleeing or fighting.

Adrenaline helps us run fast, and it helps us summon the courage to hurl ourselves at a physical assailant. But it is of zero use to us in the workplace. There is nothing a leader can do with it. Indeed, "nerves" are something every new leader gets, and must learn to overcome.

What can you do when you experience the adrenaline rush?

First, **have an emotional strategy**. Make up your mind that you will show only those emotions that advance your cause, or that don't torpedo it. You don't want to giggle at a funeral or show kindness to a bear cub in the wild. Neither can you show fear in the workplace.

Sure, terror is what you are feeling, in the pit of your stomach. But gnashing your teeth or wailing with closed eyes won't win people to your side.

When in doubt, smile. At least people will know you're trying to reassure them, which in turn makes it possible for them to reassure you. And it has the side benefit of reassuring you. If you're tough enough to put up a strong public face, you're probably tough enough to handle the new responsibility.

Take it up with your significant other. That's what mates and close friends are for—to tell your most horrible thoughts to, so no one else ever finds out about them.

Jesse, a retired professional athlete in Champlin, Minnesota, ran for statewide office as a lark, hoping to boost his public image and get a few things off his chest. To his astonishment (and chagrin), he was elected in a "perfect storm" of strange electoral conditions.

"I walked around in a daze for two weeks," he told a TV interviewer a year later. "I didn't know how to head a government. All I knew was how to growl at people and be a meatball."

Luckily, he said, "I had good people around me to help me sort it out. Best of all, my wife, Terri, was with me. I poured my heart out that night to her. How was I going to do this without making the world's biggest ass of myself?

"This is what she said to me: 'Jesse, I believe in you.' A simple thing, but it made a world of difference. But even if she'd said nothing, she was still invaluable, because I told my worst thoughts to her, not to my associates."

Head for the hills. Not right away. It doesn't look good to take a vacation as soon as you get promoted. It looks as if you're avoiding the challenge.

Instead, use a vacation as a way to ease your sense of crisis. Make a deal with yourself right now that, six months hence, you'll be going to Aruba. Make that your goal: six months of success, then a straw in a coconut.

Maybe you're not freaked. That's cool—truly cool. Not everyone responds to the call with panic. A healthy alternative is "Yippee!"

Jim, who was an orphan, worked humbly for a suburban Nashville construction firm for six months as a house painter. But his supervisors saw that he was intelligent and serious-minded, and they named him to head up an entire crew. Within a year he became head of training for the company citywide. Jim never flipped, never freaked. He expected good things to happen, because that was his nature. He did not regard advancement as a punishment from the gods.

Jim kept his cool, and that allowed his transition to leader to go smoothly.

Keep your powder dry. Here's a story showing what happens when you lose it in front of people.

Hank, an American history teacher at a high school in north-ern Ohio, was elevated to principal in an adjoining district in mid-year. Hank was a great admirer of Robert Kennedy, and when he was unsure of himself, tended to lapse into a bit of imitation. The night before he was to be introduced to the school assembly, he went over and over his speech, punching the air with two fingers to make his points. Unfortunately, when the assembly began, the kids didn't think it was as important an event as Hank did, and they were doing the usual—paper airplanes, spitballs, de-pantsing. Hank struggled through his remarks, then melted down in front of eight hundred students when he said:

"This constant fooling has got to stop around!"

You could have heard a pin drop. Then all eight hundred kids erupted in howls of derision. A simple matter of invert-ing the word order was enough to undo his career plan. Next semester, Hank was back at his former school, discussing the War of 1812.

Cheer up. After all, getting to be the leader is, for most people, not like being asked to walk the plank in a pirate movie. It's actually a pretty wonderful thing. It's a tremendous compliment. It means people know you've been doing a good job. It means higher status, higher pay, and greater satisfaction.

Many people, like Jim, are ready for this elevation, even if they have not consciously pined for a promotion. Some are "oldest children," so they are trained to have a sense of responsibility. Jim was not adopted until he was nine. That seminal experience taught him the value of patience and steady performance.

Xiaoping, a claims adjuster for a large Seattle financial services firm, was not surprised to be asked to lead a reengineering team charged with improving the claims processes. She had never set out to lead anything, but her colleagues knew she was sharp and that she cared about doing things right. She was a natural choice to lead this group, and she eagerly accepted.

The difference between Jim and Xiaoping and Josh and Bev is that leadership did not conflict with Jim's or Xiaoping's sense of themselves, their identities. Rather, it fulfilled them. Whereas, for Josh and Bev, promotion meant a major identity clash. Bev dove headfirst into a barrel of Haagen-Dazs. Josh seriously considered packing his duffel and leaving town for sunny Newfoundland.

How badly can the identity thing go? Consider the real-life story of Donald, hardware store owner in Winona, Minnesota. Donald was happy running a Coast to Coast hardware store, managing the cash register himself. But the company suggested he open a second store, and his wife, Sheila, insisted he accept the challenge.

So what did Donald do? He hired a man to murder Sheila. His sense of himself was that he shouldn't be a hardware tycoon with a raft of stores. He saw himself as being more the kind of fellow who greets customers and rings up purchases—a non-leader. Rather than go up against his sense of his own identity, he had his spouse murdered. If that sounds like the plot of the movie *Fargo,* it's because the movie was based on that story.

Now, few of us are going to reject the call to leadership as violently as Donald. But it underscores the power of how we think about ourselves, and how we let that power hold us back.

We've described two kinds of people—those who fear leadership like Bev and Josh (and Donald) and those like Jim and Xiaoping who enthusiastically embrace leadership.

But there's a third way to react, and it's actually the way most people react—it's a combination of self-doubt and delight. In all likelihood, it's the way you reacted when you first heard of your promotion to leader: pleased to be picked, but worried about succeeding.

Why are we making a big fuss about identity? Not because it is the most important issue you will face as a leader. It isn't. Issues of managerial competence, communication skills, turf warfare, and group process will all dwarf concerns about your identity.

But the identity issue is the first crisis you are likely to face as a new leader, because it hits you right away like a banana cream pie to the proboscis. For many, it can be paralyzing. For the great majority, it keeps coming back at intervals— usually in the middle of a crisis—and haunting us:

· "Am I cut out for this leadership deal?"
· "When will they find out what an imposter I am?"

It is a supremely irrational moment, and nothing we can say rationally will soothe your panicking nervous system down, guaranteed. You are having a case of the sweats, and you may just have to sweat it out.

But here's one idea: **Slow down**. No one can sustain panic for more than a few hours. The endocrine system runs out of adrenaline, and then you relax. So give yourself time to respond to this challenge. With the passage of a few days, what originally seemed unthinkable will look right up your power alley.

Here's something else you can do until the adrenaline pump runs dry.

· Make a list of your proudest accomplishments.
· Tape the list next to your monitor or phone.
· From time to time, look at the list and remember—you're pretty good at what you do.

Finally, when in doubt, remember this truth. **People aren't idiots**, no matter what you read in "Dilbert." You were picked for this challenge because someone who is not an idiot not only thought that you could handle it but that you were the best person for it.

Now is the moment to take a few deep breaths and balance the bad news with the good. No, you don't know everything you need to know to be successful with this new challenge. No new leader ever does.

But people who may know more about this than you do think you are able to learn the skills and attitudes that will ensure success.

We agree, and the following chapters will bring you closer to that success.

Three steps to establish where you are—and where you need to be:

1. **Assess your situation.** Is your assignment a piece of cake or heavy sledding?
2. **List your resources.** People, money, time, connections.
3. **List your liabilities.** What stands in the way of your project's success?

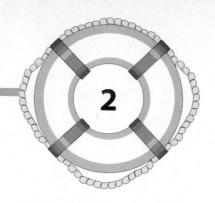

The First Day

You're lying awake, staring up at the ceiling. Tomorrow you must go in and face the people who will report to you and the people who tagged you for leadership.

And you are wondering what your chances are. Of doing a good job. Of showing the people who hired you they didn't make a mistake.

Tomorrow will be the weirdest day of your life. You will be trying to act cool and collected, but inside you a flock of giant horned butterflies will be clamoring to bust out.

How will you do? Will they turn on you and shriek, like the pod-people turned on Kevin McCarthy in *Invasion of the Body Snatchers*?

Not likely. Here's our guess: You do have some time to get settled, though not much. You have about a hundred days to prove you can handle the job. If you can demonstrate adequacy in this short period, you may have a future here. If a hundred days pass and higher-ups can see that you are as much up the creek without a clue as the day you started, your brief reign is probably nearing an end.

So the trick for you is to do the right things in the hundred days, and to yield some sign of positive results for the group you have been tagged to lead.

Don't expect everything to happen the first day. No one, not even King David, history's greatest accidental leader, ever made the leap from shepherd boy to mastery overnight. Expect your development as a leader to take place in a sequence of phases.

The first, what we call the *learning to breathe phase,* is the most difficult, and claims the most victims. It is the period of confusion and reordering that occurs in the first hundred days of being promoted. In this phase you are like red-hot metal, and the organization is the hammer and the anvil, beating you into just the right shape of pulp.

This book is mainly about that hundred-day period. Either you succeed in assembling the basic building blocks of leadership, or you fail and become organizational exhaust.

The second phase is the *competency phase,* where you learn to perform the managerial function to the point where it is no longer your Achilles heel. You become acceptable during the competency phase. Like business school, it bulletproofs you so you can be safe during a period of intense learning.

The third is the *retooling phase*. It's a feverish period of exponential growth for you as a goal-setter and redefiner. You set the table now, and you run the risks of failure. You can easily intuit that you have to go through phases one and two to even comprehend phase three.

The fourth stage then is a *looping phase* in which new learning is continuously channeled back into the experience mix, and the leader's skills and style experience incremental growth over time.

At the onset of the initial hundred-day learning-to-breathe period, the first thing you need to do is **assess just how difficult it is**, and what resources you have at your disposal. These are factors that have little to do with you personally. Exhibit 2.1 gives you a way to keep track.

Are these categories real? Yes. In fact, they occupy approximate quintiles of all organizations, each "slice" amounting to a fifth of the total pie.

Depending on which slice of the pie you work in, your task as leader is very different. A leader in the A group of Transition Friendlies will have a much easier time of it than a leader in the C group of Uphills All the Way. The main problem with leading an A organization is that people there are more accustomed to excellence than people elsewhere. They will know if you're for real or not. They will have the highest expectations of any of the quintiles.

Jean was a staff librarian with L'Ecole Polytechnique in France when he was lifted up to head the acquisitions staff of twelve other professionals. "I was astonished at how little

Exhibit 2.1. Start-Up Resources Score Sheet.

Answer these questions with a value between 10 and 0 to determine the gravity of your situation. A "10" means *totally true*, and a "0" means *you've got to be kidding*:

_____ I am part of an orderly transition, not a Saturday night massacre.

_____ The person who held this position before me will be around to help me learn the ropes. I will be surrounded by people who know what's going on.

_____ The organization is stable (no imminent mergers or acquisitions, acceptable employee turnover, no huge change initiatives like reengineering currently under way).

_____ A management system is in place to enable me to succeed.

_____ This is a quality organization known for its good hiring, good training, good products and services, and good citizenship—a leader in its field.

Add up your organization's score and double it. Here's how you stand:

81–100: **A Transition Friendly.** If you bring even modest managerial skills and a half-decent leader's personality to the game, you are enviably set up to succeed. A slam dunk.

61–80: **B Challenging but Doable.** Your work is cut out for you, but at no point will you say success is structurally impossible.

41–60: **C Uphill All the Way.** Success is possible, but it will require great effort and superior skills.

21–40: **D Transition Hostile.** The culture and systems of this organization make success difficult.

0–20: **F Dilbertia.** You inhabit an insane enterprise whose true product is the spiritual evisceration of its people.

I had to learn to run the department. This was a big surprise, because I had no experience managing anything, and I had anxieties that I would make a fool of myself. The reason? My predecessor was delightfully anal-retentive and wise, and she had set up a turnkey system for measuring progress toward departmental goals. My first hundred days were therefore very easy. In time I simplified the system and sharpened the goals to achieve greater efficiencies. But I will be grateful forever to Mme. Lafarge."

Whereas Billie-Ann, a buyer turned department store manager in Biloxi, inherited computer systems that were sputtering, staff that was turning over 100 percent every four months, and take-over rumors swamping company morale.

"I drew a line around our store, and decided we would begin with our Gulf Coast customers, making them happy to shop with us, no matter what, and the heck with the chain's prospects. We reduced the number of complaints by 38 percent in two quarters, and enjoyed a terrific Christmas season when all our other stores looked out on empty parking lots. In the spring the business was acquired by a Midwestern competitor, and several stores in the South were shut down. But not ours."

As for the lower pair of quintiles, Transition-Hostile D and Dilbertia F, you will want to **redefine success right now**. Success will probably have a paradoxical flavor, because you will be doing a commendable job in a building that is collapsing.

It may mean coming to terms with the inferior tools at your disposal. The best you can do in a D organization is sometimes to hang in there despite impossible circumstances, learning what you can, and not peeling too many years from your life expectancy.

"The sales staff at the wallpaper company had a game they called Termination," said Wally, who was hired from sales to head up a wholesale center in Santa Ana. "Termination was like a football pool, only the money wasn't on who would win on Sunday, but on what week the new manager would get sacked. We had not made a profit in twelve successive quarters, and had gone through five managers in that period. Some lasted less than two months. I remember playing Termination myself. It was a lot less fun being the guy in the bull's-eye." Wally lasted an entire year, and the company posted its first profit. But he had better places to be.

And then there is the F organization. One has to stop and ask if there is any percentage at all in being a supervisor in hell. The best leadership you may be able to provide is to extricate yourself from the relationship at the earliest opportunity.

"The culture of the place was just rancid," recalls Amos, named to head a jewelry retailer in New England. "What can I say, we sold ugly jewelry. When I tried to fire the old buyers and bring in people born after the Spanish American War, there was a revolt. The owner took their side. You couldn't get anything to happen there. If I could sum it up, it was like a bad joke that everyone kept repeating. I think if you could go to hell and come back, you'd find that it was a lot like this store. Everyone was afraid, and no one was allowed to succeed at anything."

Advice to Amos: Look for the red EXIT sign, and run, don't walk, in that direction.

Seven things you need to learn about your team members and they need to know about you—and two warnings:

1. **How long they've been with the organization**. Respect experience, but know that a fresh perspective has value, too.
2. **What they want from the team**. Money, advancement, challenge, the chance to show off? All are legitimate, but they all alter your expectations.
3. **What your expectations are**. Better they learn now than later.
4. **What the mission looks like from both sides**. Find out people's doubts and reservations. Don't try to answer them all right away.
5. **How teamwork works**. Find out who's had experience with collaboration before.
6. **What their most fulfilling work experience was**. The things people recall with pride speak volumes about what they value.
7. **What they expect and need from a leader**. You can't ask this as a direct question. Use the rest of the discussion to help you form a conclusion.
8. **Do** spend more time listening than talking.
9. **Don't** make promises you can't keep.

Meeting the Team

Now it's time to meet the team. If you already know the people who will be reporting to you, if you were a member of the team you'll now be leading, this isn't a biggie. They know you, so they should know what to expect. To screw this up, you have to go in there acting like a completely different person, confusing everyone.

Don't laugh—people do strange things when they assume new responsibilities. Kevin, a line worker at an electronics assembly plant in Bellingham, Washington, astonished his long-time acquaintances on the line by entering the meeting wearing a new suit.

"I wanted them to know they couldn't screw around with me, just because they knew me when," he explained.

Right, but it would have been better if he had removed the clothier's tag from the jacket sleeve.

Despite Kevin's experience, it is generally more comfortable to work with people you know than people you don't know.

The most important thing is to be calm. Sure, you're a bit nervous. Sure, inside you're going through a process of rushed self-appraisal. And sure, you're just starting to make sense of the promotion.

But right now people aren't looking to you for the story of your life. They know a change is in the offing, and they want to know how it affects them. This will be a good test of your leadership potential. As you meet with them, follow these rules:

Reassure them that the team goal remains in place. Even though the team leadership has flipped, the important things haven't been tinkered with or interpreted in a brand new way. This will go a long way toward stabilizing the group. The worst thing for them is unpredictable surprises based on individual differences.

Don't talk too much. You'll have a lot on your mind, but you don't want it to all come busting out at once. Now is a good time to slow down and listen to what other people have to say. It reassures them that their views are important, and that you intend to take them into consideration.

Find out what their concerns are. What better way to show you intend to lead them from their various viewpoints, than to show respect for those viewpoints? Ask them what their worries are, and do your best to assure them that their concerns are important to you.

Don't make promises you can't keep. This is an error first-time leaders often stumble into—promising to cover every bet in order to get people's support. It's one thing to promise people you'll look into matters they suggest, but it's quite another to offer blanket guarantees that you'll solve problems *x, y,* and *z*. Doing so sets you up for two opposite, equally bad things: sucking up to your team and breaking your word.

Be yourself. If they knew you beforehand, continue to be pretty much the same person. If they didn't know you, don't make someone up to be, someone more authoritative and masterful than yourself. They'll probably spot the subterfuge and laugh at you—and even if they don't, the pretense will be unbearably difficult to maintain. We'll say more about this when we talk about leader personalities.

Ten ways to feel better about your leadership:

1. Make a list of your **proven skills**.
2. **Assess your natural strengths** based on your personality type. Are you a bold entrepreneurial Doer? A sparkling Creative live wire? A meticulous, usually right Thinker? A gregarious, touchy-feelie Social?
3. Make another list, of your **unarguable weaknesses**.
4. Ask someone you trust what your **best characteristics** are.
5. **Cross-check your skills** with the task at hand. It's unlikely you are a god-awful fit.
6. Recognize that there are **some things you're good at** and some things you're not.
7. Try to take on tasks that **play to your natural strengths**.
8. **Delegate tasks** to individuals that take advantage of *their* natural strengths.
9. Assemble teams based on the **mix of talents** needed to accomplish the desired outcomes.
10. Don't **staple yourself to the cross**. Your job is to keep people pointed toward the goal. The rest—style points.

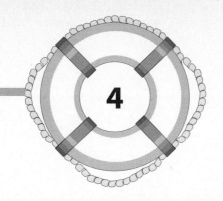

4

Deciding What Kind of Leader to Be

One of the toughest issues for new leaders is deciding how they're supposed to act. Before you were tagged for leadership, you could hide. Now, all eyes are on you. It's a bit unnerving. **Who are you going to be now**? Are you going to be a nice person, or are you going to be a slave driver?

There is probably no such a thing as a "born leader." Few of us are naturally endowed with whatever it takes to lead. Our moms and dads didn't teach us how to do it. Therefore we have to improvise a leading style. And that gets us into trouble.

The biggest mistake we make in creating a style of leading is **using the wrong model.** We ask ourselves, "Who is a strong leader?"—and the answer we come up with is often a cartoon of assertive command. Someone uncompromising. Someone who knows all the answers. Someone fiery and courageous, like George S. Patton, who perseveres in a decision long after a reasonable person would have headed for the hills.

Mel was a meatcutter in the family business in Moline until his father died, and the meat-ax of succession was passed to him. As a worker, his reputation was for being easygoing and a nice guy. But no sooner was he named manager of the operation than he sprouted a new personality, with horns.

"I became a yeller overnight, and everyone looked at me like I was Frankenstein or something. I finally figured out I felt like I needed to be that way because my old man was that way. He was an immigrant patriarch, and nobody got away with anything when he was around. I figured I had to be that way, too.

"My wife, Ginnie, who also keeps books for us, pointed out what I was doing, and she even told me why. 'Just be yourself,' she said. 'Because if you don't, I'm going to leave you, and there won't be anyone to do your books—or your laundry.' I said OK, and things have been better ever since."

The model Mel adopted was of a strict authoritarian, but it could as easily have gone the other way. He could have agonized over becoming the kind of person workers really respond to, someone they will follow out of loyalty and devotion. Then he'd have been well on his way to squandering his brief moment of leadership doing a poor imitation of Mother Teresa, being everyone's savior and defender.

Delores came from a migrant farm family, picking fruits and vegetables around the year, from Colorado to Michigan. When she was named crew chief, she suddenly became very political, sticking up for the workers at every opportunity, putting her position at risk. A grower she had known all her life took her aside and asked why she was so strident all of a sudden.

"I realized it was because I was feeling guilty about being in charge. And I didn't want the families to think I had sold out. Now, if I had lost my position, I couldn't help anybody. When I shifted gears, everyone was more comfortable. Even my brother Gustavo said to me, 'All they want is for you to tell them what to do.' He was right, but I was fighting some ancient battle in my head, going back to Cesar Chavez."

Both approaches, unless you actually are General Patton or Mother Teresa, will likely fail.

The second biggest mistake, then, is **imagining that other people care what style you follow.** Mel's butcher buddies didn't care how he worked out his Oedipal conflicts. Delores's teams didn't care about her identity struggle. They all just wanted to do their job the right way.

Sure, your people want to know what kind of boss you'll be. If they had to choose between ogre and angel, they might have a preference. But at this moment, they probably have a better perspective on your dilemma than you do. They aren't interested in your success; they are interested in the organization's success, and in achieving the goal. Because that's the outcome their jobs depend on.

Be real. The concept of authenticity becomes tiresome as everyone tells you to "be yourself." What does that mean exactly? Do the people who tell you that know who you are? Doubtful. Nobody knows who anybody is. We are complicated beings with many contradictions and cross-currents.

The truth is, you don't have to be a perfect person to be a decent leader. You can be a little nutty and be a good leader. You can be reserved and unflashy. All the types shown in Exhibit 4.1 can produce good leaders. You can be a Doer, a Thinker, a Social, or a Creative. You can be a mediocre public speaker. You can have problems matching colors and be terrible at telling jokes.

But you have to tell the truth. And people have to know that.

Talk back to your fears. Here are a few ideas that may help:

Your fear says: "What a mistake it was, recommending you for a position of authority. Once they see who you really are, you'll be out of here on your ear."

You respond: "But it's not logical that I'm incompetent. It's true, I feel some uncertainty at the moment, but I have never disgraced myself before. Chances are I will do fine with this challenge as well."

Exhibit 4.1. Four Quadrants of Success.

Thinkers	Doers
Socials	Creatives

Your fear says: "You going to get hit from every direction at once."

You respond: "No, I won't. When I name the things I'm afraid of—incompetence, failure, volcanic eruptions—it's plainly apparent that they're irrational. A reasonably bright, fair-minded person can succeed at this, and I am one."

Your fear says: "If you're so 'competent,' why are you so scared?"

You respond: "It's just stage fright. I'll get over it."

Your fear says: "Where do you get off thinking you can be as good as the leader before you, or the leaders you see around you?"

You respond: "First of all, chances are they don't always feel confident either. Second, I'm freaking out because the challenge is fresh. Give me time, and I will appear as cool and collected as other leaders appear."

Your fear says: "If you screw this up, you'll never live it down."

You respond: "Baloney. Even if this doesn't work, at least I tried. I'm a talented person and I will survive, no matter what."

Suggestion: for the first few days of your reign, **let the group goal be the leader**. It is something everyone can rally around, regardless of personality or "leadership style." Letting the goal do the leading is never bad advice. It takes pressure off you, and it focuses attention on the task at hand—which is all leadership is really about, anyway.

The next few paragraphs list a set of leadership styles. You don't have to choose a leadership style from the list, of course. It's simply a list of leader roles that have always existed, back to the cave days. But it might be wise to consider which types seem likely to feel most comfortable, for two reasons:

- It's useful to understand your natural strengths, and to therefore try to be more consistent. If you're a natural Idealist, get comfortable with the idea and be the best Idealist you can be.
- It's just as useful to acknowledge what does not come naturally easy to you. We're not saying that if you don't see yourself as a natural-born Achiever, you have to abandon all your other plans and dedicate the rest of your life to achieving great things. We are saying that if you have no knack for Achieving, you should think about that, and think of ways to stretch yourself so you can at least understand when a true Achiever comes along.

The Idealist is a true believer, led by right ideas. Idealists are valuable because they bring tremendous clarity to the task of leadership. They set precise expectations, according to the idea they hold dear, and they brook no compromise or lollygagging in implementation. The idea they are devoted to can come from anywhere—from reading, from an example set by someone else, from a set ideology or some life experience.

Idealists are dogs—their devotion to their ideas makes them models of perseverance and hard work. When Idealists are good communicators, they are terrific motivators, because they fill you with the same excitement that they feel themselves. If your team is up against the wall and needs a do-or-die effort, Idealists are great.

Idealists can run into problems, however. What if their ideas suck? What if the clarity and beauty they perceive in the idea isn't apparent to anyone else? Idealists can become nags when the idea becomes the only thing they care about. They find it easy to perceive others as foot-draggers and even saboteurs.

Accidental leaders are unlikely to include many Idealists, but you never know.

The Mentor is a people-builder, a leader who sees it as the primary function to delegate, coach, and develop people until they become, in effect, self-leading. They genuinely care about other people, and want to see good things happen for them. Mentors easily step up to accidental leadership because they are acceptable to everyone and threatening to none.

People like being around this kind of leader, because they generate such positive feelings. Mentors tend to be non-doctrinaire, flexible-minded people with an eye fixed on the long term. Because of their gifts of empathy, they are great at cultivating a spirit of customer satisfaction. If you think of the best boss you ever had, chances are you're thinking of a Mentor.

But nobody's perfect, because the fuzzy focus of the Mentor can be inappropriate in an emergency, do-or-die situation. Because they form attachments to some workers, other workers may feel they play favorites. After all, they are only human, and they tend to extend their love to people who are like them. At the remote end of the spectrum, these giving people sometimes burn out and feel that no one ever quite reciprocated with them. Sadly, some of these warm fuzzies go out in a sizzling hissy fit.

The Achiever is the ebullient leader who radiates energy and has a résumé as long as a tall man's arm. Achievers are the ultimate motivators and delegators, clear communicators and talented networkers. They get things done, and that is why they get the big money.

Achievers are good at getting the best and the most from their teams, because it is almost impossible to say no to them. Achievers are probably the single commonest type tagged for accidental leadership, because their virtues are so obvious and so attractive to superiors who want results at any cost.

On the downslope, Achievers can sometimes be a little nuts. They are prone to workaholism, which can cause them to crack up and break down, or cause you to do that, if you work for one. Also, because they are so devoted to results, they can trample people in the rush to achieve them. Also again, Achievers radiate such positive energy that they strike normally lackadaisical people as unreal or even phony. A few Achievers are so success-oriented that they have trouble with failure, and turn inside out when things don't go well.

The Innovator is the original round peg in the square hole, a person who just can't help seeing things from a slightly different perspective from everyone else. The Innovator's leadership is rooted in creativity and the pursuit of change.

It is not unusual for Innovators to be tagged for accidental leadership, because Innovators attract attention with their ideas. A single idea, folded once and inserted in a suggestion box, has launched many an accidental career.

Innovators have many gifts that blossom in positions of re-sponsibility. They bring energy, intensity, and thoughtfulness to the table. Their ingenuity can change the way a team sees itself and the spirit its members bring to their business. Further, they tend to be tolerant of other people's individuality, because they tend to be such individuals themselves.

Alas, Innovators aren't perfect, either. While they have wonderful high highs, they have low lows to go with them. No one can burn as intensely as they do, day after day. When the ideas don't come, they get depressed. Adversities that other people shrug off easily can flatten them. Worst of all, they need stimulation, and they can feel hemmed in by the policies and procedures that are at the heart of most managerial positions.

The Synthesizer is an eclectic, a thinker, a pragmatist, a "whatever works" kind of leader. Synthesizers have the gift of being able to stand back from a problem, survey great amounts of information and multiple points of view, and then determinedly make good decisions. Their great attribute is the ability to examine seemingly unrelated information and discern meaningful patterns in it.

Synthesizers aren't often tagged as accidental leaders because they seldom toot their own horns, and in lowly positions are hard to notice. They do their best work in quiet reflection, away from the give-and-take of meetings and disagreements. Their strong suit as leaders is strategy and tactics. They are careful, and reliable, and calm.

The problem with some Synthesizers is that they are too private; they lack daring and are unlikely candidates for motivational speaking. Don't look to a Synthesizer for warmth or support, or for the hard-driving exhibitionism of the Achiever. In fact, there are times when Synthesizers must be led themselves, as when they allow themselves to become too withdrawn and aloof and disrespectful of the analytical abilities of others.

The Partner is somewhat like the Mentor. Both are "people people," but while the Mentor hands wisdom down to someone younger or less experienced, the Partner is skilled at teaming with peers and working side by side with them. Partners are the consummate team players, conscientious, collaborative, and ego-free.

Think of Partners as football players, the kind that are always available to lend a shoulder, throw a block, do whatever needs doing to move the chains. Partners frequently arise accidentally because their skills and energies are on frequent display and it is impossible to object to their steadiness and modesty. A team led by a Partner will have an invincible spirit and a tight-knit, no-nonsense core.

On the other hand, Partners are prone to accusing others of not being team players and trying to oust them from the team. They may not be the most original people around, and that leads them to undervalue originality. They often insist on doing things all together. When your plane has been struck and is going down in flames is no time to be taking roll call.

The Enthusiast. Setting aside brains, a leader can have no more valuable attribute than the ability to communicate energy, and the Enthusiast has this ability in spades. Enthusiasts often become accidental leaders because their infectious passion for the task at hand is apparent to everyone. Even if they are only tagged as interim leaders, their energy as change agents will likely carry the day.

Enthusiasts are a bit like Idealists because they care a great deal about something. But that something is the mission of the group. They are consummate cheerleaders who attach themselves to the mission like barnacles. They are often a lot of fun, and in addition, they are stalwart. Long after everyone else is sick of the mission and wishes it would go away, they will still find it compelling and worthwhile.

So their strength can also be their undoing, as when they are a bad match for their team. Putting an upstart gung-ho leader in charge of a team of been-there, done-that professionals is a recipe for fragging. It takes a lot to get through to some Enthusiasts, but once you hurt their feelings, they are no good to anyone.

The Advocate has one of the strongest leadership styles. Advocates take their responsibilities very seriously. The mission becomes their client, and they will always see it through to completion. The Advocate is like a fierce guardian who protects the mission along with the team, and is willing to suffer on their behalf.

Advocates are rare birds because they are usually the most mature people in an organization, the people who know the price of things and are willing to write a check. They don't avoid conflict, and they don't mince words. Advocates take the blame when things go wrong, and spread the credit when they go right. Most team members would kill for their Advocate leaders, and the feeling is mutual.

If a team has a task that requires the best effort from everyone, their best chance is with an Advocate at the helm. Contrariwise, the Advocates' intensity is unnecessary through times of smooth sailing. Finally, their intensity can become a point of contention, as they heartily disdain the gamut of human weaknesses—dishonesty, incompetence, laziness, and complaining.

The Diplomat, our final leadership style, is as rare as the Advocate. Diplomats are genuinely wise about working with other people. Diplomats know that the person they are dealing with is as real as they are, and so they have an extraordinary capacity for respect. They are caring, and patient, and always purposeful. They are superb mediators.

Diplomats have cornered the market on a lot of old-fashioned values: moderation, excellent listening skills, a nonthreatening, low-key demeanor that puts everyone at ease, and a natural modesty that deflects attention from themselves.

Why don't we stock our organizations with Diplomats? For one thing, because people with gifts like this are rare. For another, most organizations are about as placid as a frog in a blender, and they simply don't have the luxury of putting philosopher-kings in charge, even if they can be found. Diplomats often make better counselors than leaders, because leaders are called to something even more demanding than mediation—action.

No one is bound by these types. You do not have to be one or another; nor are you prevented from being a little like several. They merely represent points on a leadership continuum of the different talents different kinds of people have had success with. And it is useful to know the strengths and weaknesses of each.

Eight things you can do to negotiate your own learning curve:

1. **Attend** conferences and workshops—about managing, about new technologies, and about your industry.
2. **Read** and pass along articles that connect to your work.
3. **Take part** in online forum discussions. Be a resource to others.
4. **Visit** related departments to find out what they do and how they do it.
5. **Talk** to customers. They know almost everything you need to know to do a better job.
6. **Reward** people who share information. Create an environment of total learning.
7. **Make** presentations to peers about your area of expertise or project.
8. **Conduct** post-mortems and post-vivums on completed projects.

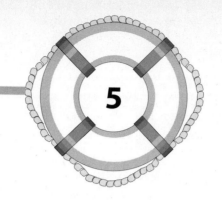

Becoming a Quick Study

All management is about learning, much of it learning that you require others to do. But a great deal is learning that you must do yourself. You need to learn

- What the mission is, and what barriers exist to achieving it
- How the existing system works, and what its weaknesses are
- Who you're working with, and what they need to succeed

This is a lot to learn, and time is limited. In truth, it's more like cramming than true learning, which allows you more time to understand the nuances of knowledge.

So how do you do it?

First, acknowledge your limitations. You cannot, in a few days, absorb the kind of detailed knowledge and familiarity with a process that your predecessor may have accumulated over ten years' time. Concede that point.

Concede, while you're at it, that there are ways you're good at learning (interviews, perhaps) and ways you're not so good (like thumbing through last year's meeting minutes). When possible, play to your strengths.

"You know how people have multiple intelligences?" asks Randy, an art director for a southeastern ad firm. "Well, I'm really good at visual and structural things, but mediocre at left-brain analysis—you know, business thinking. So when they asked me to run the team, I had a choice: admit this to myself and work around it, or hide my weakness until everyone found out about it and it was too late. It meant summoning extra will to sit down and go over weekly reports and numbers. But since I didn't expect it to be easy, I got to it more efficiently. And there was even a payoff: I think I've gotten better at doing it."

When there's learning you can't postpone, consider delegating it. Have a teammate comb through those meeting minutes with instructions to highlight passages likely to have relevance to you. Make your team part of your orientation. Indeed, make the success of your orientation their success as well.

Second, triage. Information critical to the success of the mission gets highest priority. Everything else takes a back seat.

"We had a system in avionics software where we assigned degrees of intensity to problems we were having," says Joan, who heads a new products engineering team in Washington State. "Red meant very urgent, orange meant routinely important, and yellow meant you could backburner the problem. I used this same system to flag my own education when I became interim department chief. Even when I didn't actually put a sticker on a folder, or on a tidbit I picked up in conversation,

I marked it in my mind according to its importance. It helped me focus my energies on most-crucial issues."

Surround yourself with a few good teachers, and polish their apples till they shine. Teachers are people who have skill at selecting what needs to be learned and in describing it in a memorable way. They can do so in a broad bandwidth of ways, from harsh to friendly, from didactic to Socratic, and they can dwell anywhere in the hierarchy from higher-ups to lower-downs, but they share one thing: the magical ability to make new knowledge stick.

"My teacher was my predecessor," says Christian, a business unit manager for a St. Louis–based conglomerate. "When I came in, he took me aside and told me where all the bodies were buried, who I could work with, and who I should work around. Looking back, I'm glad he retired. If he'd moved on to some other position, or been terminated, I might not have been so lucky."

Define "enough." You not only can't learn everything about everything; you really can't afford to learn everything about anything. There's just too much to know. Make up your mind before plunging into new knowledge how far you'll dive—and when you reach that depth, yank the hose.

Adopt rules of efficiency. Everything you intend to remember, write down. Some things you agree not to write down. Plan to revisit material that requires a second look.

Carmen, a sales manager in Austin, created a "yes/no" trick to help keep her mind from frying when she moved to a larger company. "Everything that came to me had to 'qualify' in my mind before I would let it in. I asked myself, 'Does this sound like something I need to know right now, or can I postpone it till later?' I even told people I was doing it, and they agreed it made sense."

As Carmen did, when someone starts a descent into a lengthy explanation of a minor detail on your first day, simply explain that you can't have that part of that conversation then. You have several options:

- *Tactful:* "That sounds like a terrific idea, and I want to get to it to do it justice. But right now I have to deal with structural issues."
- *Stern:* "That's enough for now. I'll get back to you when I can give you my full attention."
- *Pathetic:* "You should see the stack of material I have to get through by Friday."

However you frame the issue, it's a habit you must get into. There is so much to learn—if you don't put it in order, your head will assuredly pop.

Four tough questions you need to ask yourself:

1. **Why** have you been handed this assignment?
2. **What** are you good at exactly?
3. **What** are your weaknesses?
4. **How well** do you understand the challenge at hand?

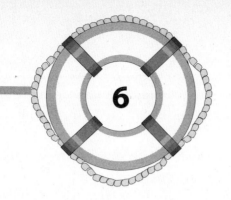

The Perfect Person
for the Job

You've scoped out the battlefield. Now it's time to inventory your ammunition and see what firepower you've got on your side to help you carry the day. Start with your own personal assets.

Self-assessment is a kind of assessment, and assessment—**figuring out what's going on**—is the leadership skill nobody talks about. Yet it is the foundation skill on which all other skills are built. Because if you don't know what you have, no change you achieve will matter because you won't be able to prove there was a change. For Point B to mean anything, there must first be a plotted Point A.

When Christopher was named head of RV sales at a Birmingham, Alabama, camper showroom, he fell apart. How was he supposed to head up a group of almost twenty salespeople, a couple of whom were working for the company before he was even born?

The first week he was on the job, he was a mess, apologizing every time he suggested an idea. Finally Bert, the vice president who tagged him for the job, invited him in and sat him down.

"Chris, what's the matter with you?" Bert asked. "As a sales-man you were poised, proficient, and predictable. You made us look good. But as sales team leader you've been like **a chicken with its head cut off**."

Unable to hold back any longer, Chris overflowed with con-fessions of inadequacy. "I'm only three years out of school. Some of these guys were pals with my dad. Jerry over there was my Scoutmaster when I was eight."

"So?"

"So, deep down, I don't think I should be telling guys like that what to do."

Bert had Chris take out a piece of paper and answer five questions:

1. Why do you suppose you were selected for this responsibility?
2. What skills and talents do you bring to the job?
3. What's the worst thing that can befall you as group leader?
4. What accomplishments are you most proud of?
5. What do you think your group should look like six months from now?

Chris struggled at first to put anything down on paper. But once the ink began to flow, so did his thoughts:

1. I was selected because I know the makes and models, and because I know the problems sales force members run into.

And because I'm smarter than most of the salespeople about financing and options.

2. I am good at understanding reports. I know how the commercial lending side works. I know the price points better than anyone. Like I said, I know the makes and models. I've probably been the best sales rep we had the past two years. And I get along with everyone pretty well. They know I'm not setting them up to fail, or trying to take credit for their work. And I'm the only person here who can get Louis off his keister and onto the sales floor.

3. The worst thing that can happen? Booting the quarterly sales targets. But that's not what I've been worrying about. I've been worrying about what the guys think of me.

4. Last April we screwed up our summer projections, and realized we had to sell three times more than we thought we possibly could. I went to management and explained the mistake. We decided to average the excess over the next eight months, a figure we thought was doable. I showed each sales rep what he had to do to succeed. When the eight months were over, every rep had made his quota. Everyone felt pretty good about it.

5. I would like to teach these people how to make their own projections, and how to make this level of performance the new norm. I figure we can do it if we give every rep a cell phone to use while traveling. That way we can change plans on the fly, if we have the latest info on customer requests.

Bert went over the questions and looked up. **"Do I need to tell you what these answers mean?"**

"No, I guess not," Christopher replied sheepishly. Bert was right. His own answers were all he needed to see his way.

Of course he was selected to lead the team. He was by far the best internal candidate, and getting someone from the outside would have meant three months of breaking in.

Of course he was shy with the older guys. But did he for a moment imagine that the sales team wanted him to screw up? No way—they were like uncles. They wanted him to succeed, big time. Even Louis.

Self-assessment is something we think we're doing all the time, but we're not. We think that little voice perched next to our good ear is the voice of self-assessment: "Oh, my, you could have handled that better." "I've heard snappier comebacks from Tupperware." "Look out for that van!"

That ain't self-assessment, that's the devil. Or someone a lot like him.

Self-assessment has to be on paper, so you can stare at it and judge its truth. (That voice by your ear, who can say?)

Write down your skills.

Write down your weaknesses.

Write down your sense of what the challenge ahead of you is.

Then, ask yourself where the gaps are—what new skills you will need, what weaknesses you will have to overcome, and what steps you will need to take to get from Point A to Point B.

Self-assessment has to be fair, and for many people that's hard, because they're not used to being fair with themselves.

Finally, **self-assessment must be strict.** A recent study on confidence and competence uncovered a frightening gap in human nature. It showed that above-average intelligent people tend to be *less* confident than below-average intelligent people.

Why is this frightening? It means that dumb people often think they are doing a great job. Obviously, they are not assessing themselves honestly, or at all.

Here's another frightening thought. The number one reason accidental leaders fail, according to Harvard's John Gabarro, is poor fit. That is, they lacked the right kinds of experience within the industry that would have allowed them to step in and move comfortably forward.

What does that tell you? For one thing, don't get too creative with your résumé. Skills learned in one industry do not readily convert to other industries. That doesn't mean you should spend your entire career in sulfur mining. But it does suggest your next step up might not be in fashion design.

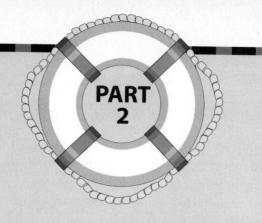

**PART
2**

Managing the
Technical Side

Five things to spend at least a week learning about:

1. **Company history** . . . how the company has changed from its origins
2. **Organizational structure** . . . who's in charge and how power flows
3. **Policies and procedures** . . . the way things are done
4. **Company scuttlebutt** . . . where the bodies are buried, and the locations of the exit wounds
5. **Financials** . . . the dollars and sense of your day-to-day doings

What They Expect You to Know, and What You'd Better Figure Out on Your Own

When you are hired or promoted, you usually get an information kit explaining key things about the organization, its structure, its mission, its benefits package, and the like.

This isn't enough. You need to learn a whole lot in a short time, and you need to immerse yourself in study and conversation to figure out the lay of the new land and what is expected of you.

Beyond the little part you are being asked to lead, you should know the **history of your organization.** You can get the sanitized outline from brochures and Web sites, describing who the founders were, what the big idea was, and how it has evolved over the years.

But you will want to go further than that, and **read between the lines.** Find out who the competition is, both traditional head-to-head competitors and the subtler kind of competition, like a new technology that could put yours out of business, or changing consumer tastes that may render you obsolete.

Where do you learn this stuff? Anywhere you can find it. Official documents will tell some of the story, especially the financials. For cultural questions, you need to talk to people, including people who have not panned out at the organization. Not to be swayed to their point of view, but to try and see the whole picture.

Find out what the company's greatest failures have been. In the process, you'll learn how it handles its failures. Are they object lessons everyone can learn from, or are they secrets swept under a thick rug in a dark corner? Where are the bodies buried?

Find out where other leaders have come from. Were they promoted from within, kidnapped from competing companies, or did people just wander in from the street?

Understand the importance of your unit or function to the whole. Are you a cash cow, a core competency, a holdover from a previous era, or an incubator for the future?

What is the retention rate in your unit? Companywide? If it's long, is it because the company is too good to people? If it's short, is it because the company doesn't know how to hold on to people? Meet a few of the old-timers and evaluate them. Do they seem like the most valuable assets in the company's knowledge base, or are they meat statues?

Understand what other units are directly affected by the success or failure of your unit. Find out who runs those units and what the relationship has been like in the past. Likewise, locate those units and functions that direct work to you, and find out how those handoffs work, and how successful they are.

Get a handle on the financials of the organization at large. If you've never studied an annual report or a profit-and-loss worksheet, now is the time to figure it out. Focus on this nexus of four statistical elements: *cash, profitability, direction,* and *market.*

Cash is an organization's food; without it, you grind to a halt, and it is very hard to get restarted. You can have great people, terrific products, and dynamite systems, but without this critical do-re-mi, you're sunk.

Profitability goes beyond cash on hand to the issue of financial viability. It is usually defined as return on assets or return on investment. At the end of the day, you have to be better off than at the beginning of the day. If your organization exists to make a profit, but its profit is no better or more reliable than an investment in a bank CD, why bother?

Direction asks if your organization is growing, stalled, or shrinking. This is controversial, but most experts feel growth is necessary to be a player in your market. The question is, How do you grow: by moving paper around, by increasing market share, by product innovation?

Finally, you need to learn your *market.* Who are your end customers, and what do they want? Don't rely entirely on focus research or statistical customer research. You need a seat-of-the-pants sense of who you're selling to today, who you'll be selling to tomorrow, and what steps your organization is taking to keep all these people happy.

Remember that the numbers are always more important than the explanations. There are many good books that help you get the basics, like John A. Tracy's *How to Read a Financial Report.*

If it's a publicly owned company, you should know this week's stock trading range and its current P/E multiple (the current value of the stock relative to the value of the company assets). So should all your reports. If the company is more closely held, examine the plan to see if targets are being met.

If it's in a conglomerate, get a bead on what role your company plays in the holding company's overall portfolio. Do you have a solid future with this outfit, or is your business a line item that can stay or go, and no one will care?

Within your group, find out what measurements are applied to track success and failure. If you're able to make the judgment—you may not be at this point—ask yourself if those measurements are relevant to today's business processes, or if they're hand-me-downs from the industrial age. You don't want to abandon yesterday's metrics wholesale. But you need to be confident that you are measuring things that really matter. Otherwise, the best plan in the world will be pointless.

Finally, **know where the power in your organization is**. Does it reside with the CEO, with the board, with a handful of owners, with the founders, with outside financial markets? Does the real power reside with customers? Does it arise from the company's own inertia—from its cash assets, its name recognition, or from policies and procedures that no one dares update?

Five measures of planning success:

1. **A goal**—where you want to go. Now is the time to define what success looks like.
2. **A vision**—to rationalize (in the best sense of the word, "to show the reason for") the goal.
3. **A strategy**—a means to achieve the goal.
4. **A set of tactics to achieve that strategy**—these are your ducks, the strategy is the row. Plan your success in big chunks (how you plan to achieve the outcomes you want).
5. **Some low-hanging fruit**—little victories you can go after first. Aim for the highest priorities that can be accomplished without great difficulty. This builds momentum and confidence that let you tackle bigger goals.

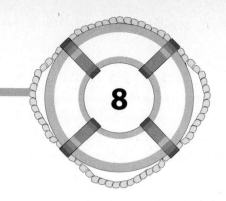

Planning to Succeed

There's no need to say how important planning is. When we attempt serious action without serious forethought, we are—what's that technical term?—oh right, *knuckleheads.*

If anything, the typical beginner's mistake is the opposite: to overplan, placing great importance on the plan and investing resources in creating it, but creating a plan that can quickly be rendered obsolete.

Why? Because it's so easy to hide behind the plan. So long as we are talking about acting and not actually acting, it isn't real. Which makes it safe. Which makes it an object of obsession.

Janet, a pediatrician in a suburban Wichita practice, banded together with two other doctors to form a start-up training company. The idea was to market a preventive health template for better musculoskeletal health for grade-school-aged kids: lessons in stretching, posture, and exercise.

The group drafted Janet to head up marketing, on the basis that she liked art and had some good ideas about logos and corporate colors. Janet proceeded to spend eight months drafting, revising, and endlessly detailing what the brochures and Web site would look like, what the market channels were, and what PMS colors would appear on company business cards. (Teal and tangerine.)

As you have already guessed, the group eventually lost confidence in Janet and simply disbanded. Janet was stunned, because the plan was getting really good about then.

And that is the paradox of planning. By nature, planning is long term. It wants to be about the long haul. But time is a killer. Leaders have only a limited amount of time in which to help their groups succeed.

The planning paradox is that a good plan takes place across a significant amount of time, but it must not forestall action. Its content telescopes outward, while its dynamic must telescope inward.

It turns out that paradoxes—contradictory truths—are awfully common in the leader business. If you try to believe both truths, you will pull yourself apart, which is all right if you are an amoeba, but otherwise is pretty bad.

You need to find a way to deal with paradoxes that does not involve tearing yourself in half. Instead of trying to separate them, try to believe in the critical parts of the two truths. Honor the paradox, and it may allow you to remain whole.

The solution here is to **learn how to do quick-shot planning**.

Quick-shot is a term from marksmanship, riflery. It's one thing to wait patiently in a crow's nest eyeing a stationary target until you can slowly squeeze off the perfect shot. It's something special to fire rapidly and accurately at a target that is moving. But that's how you must think about planning in today's crazy, continuously changing world.

What is the paradox? It is that you must shoot fast, yet shoot straight.

The secret to quick-shot planning is little victories. Your plan is not a full-scale replica of the world—where would you put such a thing even if you ever finished making it? No, your plan must be a series of moments that lead to other moments, like a flow chart of the future.

This is not as radical as it may at first sound. Any decent plan can be broken down into shorter, easily digested bites.

"We shall put a man on the moon within the decade" is a big goal requiring a massive plan. But even it can be—and must be—broken down into the requisite subsets of rocket development, manned flight training, launchpad preparation, contingency planning, and so on, each of which can be broken down into thousands of subtasks and sub-subtasks— a kazillion ducklings needing to be set in rows.

Quick-shot planning is not spray-shot planning. To succeed you need to develop an instinct for planning on the fly, for focusing on the big picture—what's important and will remain important, not what is the flavor of the day.

Piotr, a police lieutenant in the ancient city of Krakow, was promoted to head up the motorcycle division when the

previous boss was pushed aside. This happened in the spring
of 1989, as the Communist government that had been running Poland since World War II was toppled citywide by
popular vote.

His challenge was remarkable. The police force that had to
protect the fledgling democracy was the same police force that
had been oppressing and spying upon the people until a few
days earlier.

He knew what his goal was: the rule of law on the city's
throughways. But he could not know what crises lay in wait
between him and that goal. He set up his desk not in the old
chief's headquarters corner office but out in the open in
plain sight of everyone.

Over the next month he crafted a plan for keeping the best
officers and letting go those with unpardonable records.
Many obstacles were thrown in his path. By working in the
open, he convinced his cadre that he meant business and
that he intended to be open in his deliberations.

When officers objected that civil service law forbade their
firing, he changed the plan on the spot. He fired the officers
anyway, and dared them to take their terminations to court.

After two months the headquarters burned to the ground,
but Piotr stood his ground. He not only went ahead with the
firing but banished a set of five well-known "troublemakers"
from the force for life, to make examples of them.

His original plan foresaw none of these violent contingencies.
But his intuitions were perfect. *When the plan changes, change the
plan.* But hold onto the ultimate goal: the credibility of the

force. Using quick-shot planning reflexes, Piotr continuously rearranged the plan to keep the goal within sight.

Two tricks will help you know if you are doing quick-shot planning or poking yourself in the eye with a sharp stick.

One goes by the name **picking the low-hanging fruit**. Picking low fruit means you deliberately target quick wins, goals that can be accomplished with little effort in little time. No-brainers. List them out, assign them to those people you feel are best suited to getting the job done quickly. Then do it. Then celebrate the win with the whole group.

Phil, a political organizer in Winnipeg, had a problem with running a phone bank for the candidates and causes he favored. When he came to the job he was handed an exhausting document showing how to run a phone bank. But he could see people were becoming deeply discouraged only ninety minutes into a calling session. People were yelling at them, and the huge numbers of remote and implausible possibilities on their call lists made the work seem like, well, being in hell.

Phil culled the lists so that the first ninety minutes were likely to include at least a half-dozen qualified names—people who were likely to say yes or donate money. It worked. Callers got early reinforcement and volunteered for another day. They also got experienced in the art of bothering people during the dinner hour. Once the volunteers inured themselves to their own rudeness (in the name of a cause they championed), they became good telemarketers: the kind we love to hate. And Phil's candidates got elected.

Picking low-hanging fruit is more than just a planning tactic. It's a way to give your team or group an early win, something to high-five about, thus encouraging them to think that winning (under you!) is not just possible but darn near inevitable.

But it is an intelligent plan-making device, too, because this early energy will get you off to a good start. And it reminds you that, in the execution of a plan, your horses will need to drink from time to time.

The other trick is called goal stacking. *Goal stacking* is a way to sort through all the demanding and conflicting needs a team seems to face at the outset of a plan. It means tagging those short-term tasks that deserve prioritization and tackling them in order of priority. It is a powerful way to sort through what really matters, and what is just cluttering up the plan.

Nicole ran a driver's license bureau in Lyons. Her long-term goal was to convert licensing from a mail-run, analog license process to an e-mail—run, digitized image process. Using new technologies, she pledged to cut the process from sixty days to one week. She gave the department six months to achieve this speed-up.

She sorted the different elements of her plan into three distinct time frames:

- *Short-term* goals were those that must be accomplished in the next month (even shorter if possible).
- *Mid-term* goals were those that needed to get done in anywhere from one to two months.
- And *long-term* goals were those that must be completed in anywhere from two to four months.

Nicole solved the problem sooner than she expected, by breaking the process down. She learned the importance of

prioritizing, of selecting the right task to address at the moment.

She found, for purposes of effectiveness, that the most important priorities were those in the short-term range. She listed them from the highest priority to the lowest priority, and she made sure her people knew what these priorities were.

And the department responded. They mastered the technology in less than two weeks. They managed to troubleshoot the various glitches and hold-ups in another two. They communicated the new process to the public for much of the next six weeks.

The department came to be driven by this looping stack of short-term priorities. If a deadline passed, the priority was fed back into the stack and tried again, with a different deadline.

After three months she noticed something. Some things just never got done, no matter how many times she listed them as priorities.

The lesson Nicole learned: the uncompleted priorities were not high priorities. After a while, she gathered an armful of these short-term priorities and threw them in the trash. And the department made the conversion deadline—her first big challenge as a leader—with two months to spare.

Intuitively, Nicole grasped what we all need to learn: that leading and planning requires implementive discretion, to assign priority to tasks—and to strip priority away. Goal-stacking is an important tool in your quick-shot planning tool kit.

Successful leaders focus their group's efforts on completing high-priority short-term goals. **Think bowling**. In bowling the object is to knock down as many pins as possible per frame. You only get ten frames to do this. (As a new leader, your ten frames translate to roughly a hundred days.) You don't have a moment to waste on lower priorities.

Get together with your group at least once a week to discuss the priorities you are working on that week. Keep the plan flexible and able to give so you can all focus on the highest, shortest goals.

Then celebrate with the team. Bowling is a nice way to celebrate, because it's so silly. And the next day, when you all get back to work, hang onto that image of bowling. What are today's highest short-term priorities? Take aim and knock them down.

Six stages of bringing an idea to completion:

1. **Catalyzing.** The initiating task of leadership: bringing an unperformed idea to concrete fruition. Change starts with a single individual and then fans out, acquiring its own life in the organization.
2. **Encoding.** Before people can subscribe to an idea, they must understand it. Communicating the necessity of the change is the leader's job. Communicating is the hardest task of leadership, because it's so easy to do it badly. The danger in the encoding process is that the act of preserving it will also embalm it.
3. **Imagining.** Imagining happens when the leader's words form a picture in people's minds. What was not visible now comes swimming into view. The first sign of success is when a critical mass of people share the vision and subscribe to it.
4. **Uniting.** Like dominoes, other people fall in line behind the idea, giving it momentum. Leaders obtain commitment and support both formally and informally. Dissenting views are met halfway, heard, respected, and responded to.
5. **Fitting.** All the leader's systems for measurement, hiring, training, communications, development, rewards, and operations advance the idea rather than weight it down.
6. **Gelling.** (Not hardening!) Leadership drives the change down through the team, challenging everyone to make it a part of their thinking.

How a Little Orderliness Can Extend Your Shelf Life

You've assessed your challenge. You've drawn up a plan. (Well, what you really did was adopt a philosophy of versatile planning and filled in a few lines that lead to your goal.)

Now it's time to divvy up duties. It's an awesome moment, when you find yourself for the first time acting in opposition to your team's preferences.

"I went into our first team meeting with everyone congratulating me on the promotion," said Satijat, a software development team leader in Mumbai. "I was very pleased and proud. But when the hour was up, I saw every person leaving with eyes cast down. It was apparent to me that the relationship had altered significantly."

This process has three aspects: roles, responsibilities, and accountabilities. Your job as leader is to decide

- Who does what
- When they have to finish it
- What happens if they mess up

This is the very guts of management: getting people to do things. Succeed at this, and the whole world will doff its cap when you pass by. Just as likely, however, you'll struggle with yet another paradox, getting human beings with free will to do your will.

This is where the word *organization* comes from: putting chaotic human elements together in such a way that they behave in an orderly, predictable fashion. Through history, the best way to do this by far has been **brutality**. If subordinates can't be persuaded with sweet logic to follow instructions, a few turns of the thumbscrew usually ensure compliance.

Apart from a few industries, that approach doesn't fly in the modern world. Which leaves managers with the dicey task of moving people who all start out with some level of resistance to order, to order.

People have many reasons to resist, and you cannot expect your powers of persuasion, or lack of same, to pry people loose from their private convictions. Some reasons for resistance:

- What you want them to do is not what they want to do.
- What you want them to do violates their sense of who they are.
- They did not join your team in order to obey your whim.
- They joined your team because they had to.
- They joined for personal glory.
- They joined because one aspect of the work intrigued them.

- They joined to be with or near someone else in the group.
- They joined to escape some other group.
- They joined because you're new, and they think they can get away with murder.

You must learn quickly that people are not putty in your hands. They come to the work with their own agendas and their own needs. Until you acknowledge this natural diversity of motive and bring your group beyond that stage, leading will be like juggling cats. They will always frustrate you.

Otto, newly named warden of a medium security confinement facility in Massachusetts, had never run a correctional facility before. But his background as a psychologist stood him in good stead. In his first week at the prison, he held a get-to-know-you session with his management team that began with Otto serving brats and beer, followed by karaoke singing, followed by a bitch session at which everyone was encouraged to talk about the prison, their career frustrations, and what they really wanted to see happen.

The brats and karaoke were ways Otto got people to relax, so they could be honest for the final part of the evening. He learned more that night than most managers learn in a year. Who was considering a transfer, what the perfect prison would be like, and what constituted the perfect mix of duties.

Before the evening ended, however, Otto dropped a bomb.

"I'm not here to make all your dreams come true, or to change your job descriptions so you're just doing the things you enjoy. **This is a prison**, and some of what we do is pretty unpleasant.

"But I'll make you this promise. I will treat you as fairly as I know how. And I will listen to every word you tell me. I want each and every one of you to succeed here. If you want to be somewhere else, I'll work with you on that, too. But first, we have a job to do, and nobody is excused."

You could have heard a flea fart. But Otto had made his point. He respected where people were coming from. Individual needs were acknowledged. But now people had to come together and get behind the mission. And they did.

Getting organized is a treacherous moment. One false move, and the team is doing the leading and goal-setting, not you.

There are two things you should especially watch for at this stage, for they have the power to snuff out your effectiveness like a candle.

The first is turf anxiety. Turf battles occur when two people want to do the same task, and have the same responsibilities. You see it in government all the time, where the secretary of state and the national security adviser perceive that they have the same job, and are forever at one another's throats. Sometimes it is the result of vague job descriptions that list the same task for two people.

An Oregon-based technology conglomerate hired two vice presidents of marketing, one for the corporation and another for the company's largest division. Then it compounded matters by locating both of them on the same continent—worse, just down the hall from one another. For years they battled over which of the two "set the table" for the other. The CEO was culpable: he thought it was a healthy thing to pit them against one another. "Make it a competition to see who has the best ideas," he said. But it was a waste of creativity, and wound up shortening both women's careers.

The trouble with turf is that people are protective of it. Ask someone to surrender turf, and they are not likely to comply without a stink. Ask someone to share turf, and you have set the stage for a battle, and it will be a battle royal, because people take turf *very* seriously.

Are overlaps always a bad thing? No, provided people have room to work within the contested turf. When two people are willing and able to work together to overcome any differences of opinion, overlaps work. Mostly, though, they result in pointless competition, in a waste of spirit and imagination and not in constructive collaboration, and should be avoided. When people don't feel safe to do their jobs, you've got trouble.

One way to defuse a turf battle is to confront the contestants and ask them what they think they're fighting for. Ask each person why the job is worth having. This shifts the focus from a death struggle to new possibilities. There's never a shortage of important work to do; so why fight over it?

You may discover that the paired antagonists can work together after all. One may make a mentor for the other, and pass the turf on in time. Or perhaps there's one part of the task that really fires up one or the other, and it can be divided without bloodshed.

The point is, turf is real, turf battles can get fierce, and you don't have the time to screw around with one.

So much for fiercely coveted assignments. **The other trouble spot is the opposite, the job no one wants, the hot potato.**

A hot potato is scut work, taking out the garbage, the boring paperwork, any of the nasty jobs that satisfy none of our higher yearnings.

Nevertheless, someone has to do them or the overall goal cannot be met. Call your team together and announce you need a volunteer to reconcile team expenditures to budget allocations, and watch your soldiers scatter.

Two bad things can happen.

- One, no one volunteers and the necessary but mind-deadening work does not get done, the project fails, and you all end up in the unemployment line, volunteering for the scuttiest jobs available, and happy to be assigned one.
- Two, the wrong person takes on the hot potato. You hand it off to a team martyr—a passive-aggressive type who is happy to take such assignments on, only to turn around sixty days later and complain bitterly about being taken advantage of. How bad is this? Team martyrs, because they don't speak their minds until it is too late, are the people who go crazy and shoot the rest of the team. Talk about a goal-killer.

Come on, you know the answer to the hot potato predicament: identify all the unpleasant but necessary assignments and continuously rotate them among all your people; say, every thirty days or so. Everyone takes out the garbage when it is their turn, even the star performers.

Keep in mind that when assigning work, try your best to take advantage of people's natural strengths and skills. Now is not the time for personnel development. Training for yourself and others can come later, after you've got a good start and feel comfortable in your leadership role.

Now a few words on the nature of order.

Getting organized isn't about building a box, a perfect machine that never fails. Too often we hear the word *organize* and think there is some static condition of perfection called *organized* in which things never go wrong.

There are no perfect boxes in the business or nonprofit worlds. Managers, who by definition are makers and maintainers of boxes, tend to underestimate the oppressive powers of chaos and entropy. Things fall apart, they wear down, they head south on you. Get over it.

Organization does not mean keeping your desktop clear and polished. It means creating an environment in which good things happen. It can often appear quite disorganized—but the work gets done.

Better than clearing your desk is to clear out your head. You need to be uncluttered to be effective. That means clearing the deck of things that belong on a list, or a Rolodex file, or a chart, or a spreadsheet, and freeing your gray matter to do the real work of leadership—describing goals, coaching people on how to achieve them, paying attention to their progress, and intervening when necessary.

A better impulse, to our thinking, is to look at the word *organized* and focus on the *organic* part. A team is less a machine than a living thing. Tend to it as you would a rose bush, and you just might get roses.

Nine things you can do to bring people into your circle:

1. **Spend time with them**. Time is the new money, an investment whose sincerity no one can mistake.
2. **Listen to them**. Listening is more than facing people and nodding your head until it's your turn to say something. Other people know things you don't know. If you pay close attention, you will find things out that will amaze you.
3. **Appreciate differentness**. You need people you can trust who aren't afraid to disagree with you. Remember, you have no time for pussy-footing—cut to the chase, even if it means getting trampled emotionally. You will last a lot longer if you have at least one friend you can count on for support—not a yes-person, but a you-person.
4. **Thank them**. We talk about win-win dealmaking. But thanking does deeper. It means ritually acknowledging that they helped you, and you are in their debt. If you really want to sweeten the deal, thank them in front of other people. Genuine gratitude makes people feel better than heroin. Fewer side effects, too.
5. **Keep your ears open**. You'll be surprised at the good things that fly in. After all, no leader leads alone. You can't succeed if you spurn the help and advice that others naturally provide.
6. **Team up**. Partner with peers, supervisors, and subordinates. Let people know you are available to them. This induces "interpersonal reciprocity"—it greases the skids.
7. **Be direct**. You won't get help unless you ask for it.
8. **Look for human gold in the mine**. That is, find people in your organization who have worked in your department in the past and can provide input.
9. **Join associations**. People who do similar work naturally share information and learn from one another, create bonds, and provide help when asked.

Who You Can Turn To

N̲o one leads alone. Sure, we're accustomed to those grim pictures of top executives, gazing out their office windows, their faces careworn from the burdens of the job. It's lonely at the top, the pictures seem to say.

But those photos—generally taken by staff photographers, for public relations purposes—depict responsibility, not loneliness. Leaders who do their jobs are continually consulting with others.

They are always plugged in to other people. They use others as mentors, as peer review panels, as confidants to bounce ideas off. They schmooze, they copy, they complain, they listen, they steal. Sometimes they just turn their dials down and relax with friends. Leading is a very social function, or you're not doing it right.

Why do so many new leaders feel they have to go it alone?

One reason is that they want to seem pure—uncontaminated by cronyism or favoritism. Another reason is pride—they feel that unless the ideas and decisions are 100 percent theirs, then they get no credit for success. A few may even feel that it is un-adult to turn to others for help when they are the ones in charge; a very un-adult attitude, if you ask us.

One overlooked fact about leaders is that they are not God. Every leader reports to someone else; even CEOs must report to boards, to shareholders, to customers, to regulators. No leader is an island!

Who decided you were capable of running this operation? Chances are that someone, somewhere in your organization, had a vested interest in your success, and that's why you were chosen to lead.

It may be because they like you, or it may be that *their* success hinges on *your* success. Whichever it is, these persons should be an invaluable resource to you, for running interference, providing information, taking the blame, and averting retribution.

We call them *lifelines,* because that is what they are to you—heroic resources connected to a dotted line, possessing remarkable superpowers within an organization. They can be fantastic. They can also be threatening, as when, as sometimes happens, a lifeline wants to make you into a pet chinchilla.

"When I was invited to move to Tacoma to head up station marketing, I didn't know anyone west of Akron," said Steve, formerly an independent broadcasting consultant. "The only person I had any kind of relationship with was the owner, who was no longer part of management, but who still exerted a lot of influence. He was the reason I got hired. He met me at a confab the previous fall and jotted my name down.

"So when I got there, he took me out to lunch almost every day and filled me with his views on how the station needed to change. Basically, he wanted to take it back to the 1950s. I knew that his views were eccentric, but how could I stand up to him when I owed my job to him? Meanwhile, everyone I worked with thought I was his fair-haired boy. It took me eighteen months to step out from under his shadow. And when I finally did that, he was sore at me. It was a mess."

You can benefit from a protector while signaling your independence, but you must do it early in the relationship. Make clear your gratitude, and if necessary, throw your protector a low-cost bone. Steve, in Tacoma, agreed to retain a local morning kids' show that was a favorite holdover of the owner's. Ratings were so-so, but the show was in its sunset era anyway, with the host in his seventies and no replacement in sight. "I figured it cost me very little, and it made Eugene happy. Which freed me up to do a total makeover of local news."

Lifelines are only the beginning. **You need allies inside and outside the organization.**

First, the insiders. You are continuously surrounded by others who can, over time, become either your enemies or your allies. We call these people *partners*. Whether you are looking upwards, sideways, downwards, or outwards, you'll see people willing and able to partner with you for mutual success.

Seek out those who have political clout in your organization to help you remove barriers (or at least advise you where the

barriers exist). Seek out those with more exposure to the organization—the grayhairs who've seen it all. Seek out higher-ups
who are willing and motivated to coach, counsel, and mentor
you; not just for that first hundred days but after you've become more at ease with leadership.

Once you locate these partners, you've got a big challenge:
getting them to help. People are often willing to lend a hand
if asked. But they are poor mind-readers. Don't expect them to
know what you want just because you're standing in front of
them with those big puppy-dog eyes.

Smart leaders know that no one makes sacrifices for the sake
of being a good person. (Well, there are a few persons who
appear to be doing this, but be very afraid of them, because
one day after years of selflessness they will expect payment,
and it will be *ugly.*)

With rare exceptions, however, **few people work against
their own self-interest**. An important part of the leader's
job, therefore, is to find out what people want, and make
deals with them. Find out what defines a win for others.
(You can assume they're all asking, "What's in it for me?")

It could be attention or a promotion. It could be an opportunity to try an idea out. It could be a personal favor. It could
be help with their career. It could simply be an occasional
smile and a pat on the head.

You may not always want to pay the asking price. ("Never tell
anyone what I am doing with petty cash.") Asking prices can
be compromising, and you do not want to commit yourself to
something that is unethical, or uncomfortable, or unfair.

But the secret to win-win thinking is to keep looking for ways to gain cooperation from people. Because once you establish an asking price that you don't mind paying, you're in business.

Finally, outsiders. Outside the organization, it's useful to have people to confide in who share common interests with you. Someone from another organization—a completely different industry—a special interest group or association.

What's great about these folks is that you don't owe them anything. You can ask them questions and share stories you would be embarrassed to bring up in front of your own team. Lean on one another. **Become mirrors for one another, giving honest feedback and counsel.**

"We had a new leaders' group at our local chamber of commerce that met on the third Wednesday of each month to talk about problems," says Stan, an assistant manager with a retail shoe chain in Chicago's north suburbs. "Everyone was in a different business, but everyone was going through the same thing. I made a couple of friends there that I still get together with, three years later."

We suggest you cultivate a handful of people you feel comfortable with. Make it a regular thing—you will benefit from the camaraderie. Don't be afraid to form friendships with people from the other gender, or other age groups, either. The main bond between you will be that you understand and sympathize with one another's plights—not that you like the same music.

Seven ways to get out of the box, and stay out:

1. **Don't get trapped behind your desk**. Schedule time on your daily calendar (twice a day minimum) to wander around and talk to people on their home turf.
2. **Ask team members regularly what you can do to help them**. Don't wait for them to come to you.
3. **Question everything**. Take nothing for granted, not even the most conventional wisdom.
4. **Meet with other team leaders** to see how your team integrates (or doesn't) with the organization.
5. **Find resources outside your immediate organization**. You never know where you'll come across something that might help your team accomplish good outcomes.
6. **Let others know what your team is doing**. (Go for publicity both inside and outside the organization.)
7. **Use the right metrics**, or you'll get the wrong results.

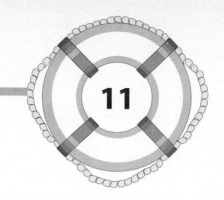

Set Fire to Your Credenza

The difference between managing and leading is that managing is done in a box of predictable inputs and outputs, and leading happens out in the open, where weird and unpredictable things are the order of the day.

This distinction does not sound like a recommendation for leading. Who wouldn't prefer a fixed system to run, a place where you can close your door, roll up your sleeves, and do your job in connect-the-dots fashion?

Alas, your office is not your workbench. Think of it as a place to hang your coat and make phone calls. **Most of the time, you should be out**. Out of the office, out of the box. A great danger of leading is slipping into a too-easy groove.

Doubtless you have heard of MBWA, or "managing by walking around." The idea is simple: you can't understand how well a process is working unless you are close to it. Most managers honor the idea by making regular forays into the operational arena, speaking with workers, and letting them know the boss is on the prowl. A few use it as a way to surprise workers in the act of being themselves, as a managerial gotcha.

Roaming around is about doing a better job, not getting a breath of fresh air. But it has a galvanizing effect on everyone it touches. Some employees will be nervous: "The boss is coming!" But the point isn't for you to be in their face; it's for them to see your face and realize you care about how things are done.

All that is to the good, but we suggest a more subversive level of wandering: not just to physically move about, but to adopt a continuously wandering mentality, a curiosity about all things.

Things to check out in your peregrinations:

- What do teammates really think about stuff? Engage them not just in scheduled meetings but in one-on-one conversations, over a beer even. You desperately need to get honest input from your key people, including those sacred areas where people are afraid to speak the truth.
- What's going on in other units in the company? Have they figured out efficiencies and economies that would take you years to arrive at on your own?
- What's the word in the larger community? In your reading? Among competitors in your industry? Among companies in other industries? Wander down to the library, the local Chamber of Commerce or Rotary Club meetings. Go where you have to, to escape from the box.

Glenn, a Boston-based insurance executive, sees himself as a kind of organizational mole or double agent, spending well over half of his time walking around, talking to workers, uncovering problems or perceptions of problems, and then challenging his senior managers to come up with solutions. When an employee resigns, Glen personally reads through the transcripts of the exit interview to find out what made the person want to leave.

Alicia, promoted to a management position based on the energy she exerted as a travelers assistance rep at an international airport in a western state, is virtually never at a desk. With her cell phone headset in place, she is out and about almost every minute of the day, interacting with travelers, skycaps, baggage handlers, and assorted airport personnel. She is so frenetic in her outreach it is almost off-putting. But Alicia won't let you be put off for long. She gets people involved, one way or another, either directly by collaring you and hitting you up for ideas or resources, or indirectly, by using you as a model.

It's easy in a small, single-site business. In multi-site organizations, roaming around presents an interesting challenge: **How do you roam around when the "around" is transglobal**? The answer: You walk when you *can* walk, and you use other means when you have to. E-mail is a great way to poke your head across an ocean and six time zones and say hello.

Roaming is not for the squeamish. The entire point of it is to see things you would otherwise not see—to "walk on the wild side." It requires that you feel comfortable about not feeling comfortable.

Six ways to create a learning environment:

1. **Read** articles and books about leadership.
2. **Attend** conferences on leadership.
3. **Talk** with other leaders about what they find difficult and how they handle these situations.
4. **Seek** a mentor—someone in a leadership position who will volunteer to provide you with guidance and advice.
5. **Join** associations on management and leadership and attend their luncheons.
6. **Learn** from your mistakes and the mistakes of others.

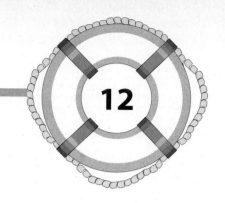

Leading by Learning

I n Chapter Five we looked at the learning you must do to be a leader. This chapter is about the learning that you as leader must get *other people* to do.

Step back from the individual tasks of business and they all look like instances of learning:

Communicating the mission is learning. Planning makes the mission learnable. Managing is expediting people's efficiency at learning how to do their jobs. Negotiation is a kind of two-way learning in which both sides arrive at fresh understand-ing. Teams are cross-functional learning engines. Quality is the ability to measure results, learn from them, and adapt.

So a serious leader has a serious attitude about learning.

Some organizations flaunt their commitment to learning, utilizing vast and proprietary knowledge management capabilities to churn old knowledge into new applications, and to transfer knowledge from one head into the heads of many.

Such organizations are like a dream come true for accidental leaders. Instead of hoarding knowledge, people throw it at you. The trick is being able to catch it.

Most organizations, however, are pretty iffy about learning. They typically farm training out to subcontractors. Invariably, when hard times come, training budgets are the first thing to go. And then they wonder, when the economy improves, why their competitors seem quicker to innovate and deploy.

Chances are, your company doesn't have a multimillion-dollar training facility. What can you do then, as a new leader saddled with an old culture of training, to develop a learning spirit within your team? First, understand that **learning and training represent diametrically different approaches to solving business problems.**

Everybody knows what training is. Employers identify shortfalls in what employees know—what ISO 9000 is, what common causes are, what a feedback loop is and how to keep one open. Then they do whatever they have to do to get that information into the employee's head. *Training* is symbolized in college coats of arms with the medieval icon of a lamp of knowledge pouring its oil in the passive student's ear.

Though training is a $100 billion industry and a vital item in every organizational budget, it is typically concerned with the humdrum how-to side of organizational affairs—how to do quality, how to do JIT, how to do business process reengineering. Training defines itself as an information delivery system. Whether it is conducted by people in classrooms or on the job, or by machine in the form of videotape or multi-media CD-ROM, it is a static, measurable thing that brings employees up to the present desired state, as defined by management. It is not a desired thing by itself; it is a means to an end.

Learning is almost the opposite of training. It is not a "business," yet it is everyone's business. Though it makes no one any money, it allows people in an organization to draw nearer to objectives. It happens entirely in the learner's head, and requires no technology whatsoever. It is by its very nature unmeasurable and undefinable. **Learning is an end in itself, not a means to an end**.

The two are seldom spoken of together, but they are the two charged rails of change. One pushes ("Now hear this!"); the other pulls ("What do you think?"). No organization can leave the station without a determined effort to continually increase its knowledge base.

But the two are often at odds. Training wants to cover the greatest amount of ground in the shortest time, with the fewest interruptions and the highest degree of learner homogeneity. It wants above all to be finished and get paid. Learning, by contrast, knows no clock, respects no formal structure, and occurs in as many ways and at as many paces as there are learners.

A lot of lip service has been paid to "the learning organization," a phrase coined by Peter Senge in *The Fifth Discipline*. In the Senge view, the long-term goal of any organization is not making and selling more and more widgets, but managing the knowledge process that allows the company to continuously discover better ways to meet the needs of its widget customers.

Focusing on training as an end unto itself is great for the training company, but maybe not so great for your team. All the value for your organization is concentrated at the learning end of the horse, not the training one.

Training is product. It is what you shop for. Learning is process, the goal of the training. As your organization grapples with its change initiatives, you will want to run reality checks to make sure you are inducing *learning* and not just providing training. A checklist like this one will come in handy:

Do you know exactly what knowledge you want to see increased? Is it generic, like statistical process control or ISO 9000, or specific to your industry, like restaurant service quality management? Do you have that knowledge yourself? Are you competent to evaluate that the transfer has been done well? How well does the program you are looking at mesh with your needs? Is it efficient—does it overdo or underdo? Something can be a great training tool for someone else but the pits for your group.

Did the training overcome workers' objections to it? We've all got bad attitudes, especially when the presumption is that we don't know something. Good training does something from the very outset—uses humor, gets people involved, explains why the training is good for the organization and for the learner—to knock the chip off learners' shoulders.

Was there at least some kind of human component? The sales pitch of the person who sells it to you isn't enough. Everyone needs a hand to hold at some stage. It may include facilitation, consultation, installation, customization, tech support, or training of trainers. Even a 24/7 online knowledge base can embed a level of human interaction (albeit a cold one) to relieve the mechanical flow of information.

What will be the outcome of the training? What proof will you have that the training "took"? Testing is the answer, either formally, with pencil and paper, or informally, by evaluating subsequent behavior. Online tutorials teaching ISO 9000 or quality techniques are wonderful in that they self-test on the fly. A learner who is learning how to cut and paste, for instance, cannot go on to the next lesson before demonstrating actual cut-and-paste skills.

What happens next? Is the training product a one-shot deal, or will you want to turn to the same source for repeat sessions or extension products? Is it important to develop a longer-term relationship with the trainer as a sort of strategic partner? Or is it, *Seeya later, facilitator?*

Successful training does more than pour information in people's ears. At its best it engages the learner's imagination, triggering a positive change in behavior that pulls toward greater organizational success. When training does this it crosses the boundary to learning.

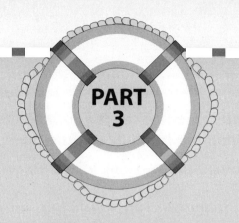

Managing
People

Six things to remember when your team is hovering on the brink of dysfunction:

1. **It's not true that teams don't work**. It is true that many teams don't work.
2. **Leaders must learn when a project calls for a team solution**. Some tasks are best left to an individual. Others—when the outcome will affect a cross-section of the organization or the effort will require input from multiple sources—work best in teams.
3. **Take time to figure out what needs to get done by teams and what by individuals**. Make a list for each.
4. **Assign a team** and a team leader for each team-based outcome.
5. **Meetings help**. Have members of your team meet with others both inside and outside your organization who could be used as team resources.
6. **Encourage your team members to join trade associations (and attend the meetings)**. The helping networks they build will make a big difference to them and to the success of the whole team.

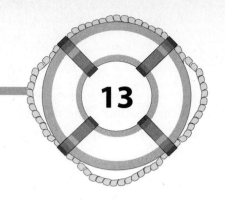

Living with Teams

Are teams necessary? For the accidental leader, the question is self-answering: If your job is to lead a team, teams have to be necessary. Or you aren't necessary.

But if you're to be a good team leader, you need to understand when teams work, and when you're better off doing without them.

Teams have been around since hunters first ganged up on mastodons. But teams in the modern sense, of people with different skills coming together to perform a common task, are relatively new.

The beauty of a good team is that it is efficient: people self-organize without a lot of bureaucracy. A good team saves money for the organization by being lean and fast and productive.

But sometimes we go overboard with the concept and demand that everything be done on a team basis. When that happens, one bureaucracy replaces another. The challenge for the accidental leader is to **know when to apply a team to a task, and when to keep things simple**.

To do teams right, you need to be constantly checking their oil and tires and making sure they're functioning as intended. For speedy team diagnosis, here is a handy checklist of the signs that teams leaders are in trouble:

People are frowning a lot. Teams are herky-jerky things, because while they are ostensibly about achieving the stated team goal, they are invariably made up of individual team members working on individual goals. The goals can be about career advancement, spending more time with family, working alongside appealing people, getting strokes for doing good work. Team members want all sorts of things besides achieving the team goal. The smart thing to do is get to know one another early on, and get those "unmentioned agendas" on the table. It helps people appreciate one another better and sharpens the focus on the team goal.

People seem muddled. Sometimes the leader is too nice, or too vague, or the team goal is contradictory. Whatever the reason, team members aren't sure what they're supposed to do, or it doesn't make sense to them. The leader has to identify this confusion early on and do whatever is necessary to dispel it. Sometimes it means getting a clarification from higher up. Sometimes you're screwed, because the goal really is a mess—and intends to go on being a mess. The earlier you find that out, the better.

People are empowered to dig their own graves. It's no good to have the power to make decisions unless that power is carefully defined. Don't let team members spend $1 million on their say-so. Set quantifiable limits to their powers, and you will all sleep better at night.

People feel discouraged. They feel there's no way they can make headway as a team because the organization as a whole is so primitive that they're imprisoned in a mountain of ridiculous policies and procedures. The solution is to become guerrillas and to serve the team goal first and the company rules second.

People are stabbing one another in the chest. In any group there are going to be conflicts. The leader's job is to keep squabbles from undermining the team effort. Most conflicts can be resolved with a friendly conversation or warning. Severe differences may require separating individuals. Really severe differences call for permanent separation.

People think you're a turkey. If your leadership is tentative or inconsistent, the goal will die. You must figure a way to serve the team and keep the vision alive. If you can't do this, leave now.

People need their glasses wiped. It isn't their vision that's failing, it's the organization's. "Having a vision" is no great feat; Captain Ahab had a vision. Have the *right* vision, and express it in the terms it deserves. And keep expressing it over and over until it catches fire in people's heads.

People are under siege. Lots of times companies switch to teams, but they don't uproot their own anti-team attitudes.

Who wants to work at a place where the culture virtually screams out, "We don't want you here!"

People don't know from squat. Performance isn't being measured; team members are groping in the dark. The solution is to create a discreet system of useful information flowing to and from all team members.

People are getting the short end of the stick. Are you rewarding people for teamwork, or is the old every-man-for-himself system still in place, behind the team rhetoric?

People don't believe a word you tell them. A team without trust is like a vampire victim. If you're the reason trust has drained away like blood from the corpse, shame on you. Of all the calamities that can befall a team, this is the most fatal.

People don't give a hoot. Your team knows the goal, they've heard your spiel, and they just don't feel like complying. Probably time to get a new team.

There's a bottom line to teams, and it's this:

Use them when they work, and when they don't work, use something else. Remember that what you are usually after is not a structure ("cross-functional self-managing team") but a *result* ("getting the job done").

For that you need teams less than you need the spirit of teamwork. Cultivate cooperation and sharing, weed out the turf issues and ego games, and you'll have 99 percent of the team you need.

Five rules for successful succession:

1. **Never badmouth your predecessor**. Everyone's got good and bad behaviors. Speak well of your predecessor's past accomplishments and forgive the shortcomings you notice in the hope that others will forgive yours.
2. **Set your own expectations**. Make sure your staff all know what you want.
3. **Find out what has worked and what needs fixing**. Talk to your staff.
4. **Make an agreement** to work with your staff to meet your expectations.
5. **Never forget:** You are in charge.

Packing Up Your Predecessor

The classic accidental leader was Jerry. In 1973 he was minority leader of the House of Representatives, with no particular reputation for legislative skills or policy astuteness. But when Vice President Spiro ran into ethical problems, President Dick lifted Jerry up, to Jerry's great astonishment, to be Dick's likely successor.

Within a year, when Dick became the first American president ever to resign his post, the accidental vice president was sworn in as **accidental president**.

Jerry was widely perceived as incompetent, going back to President Lyndon's earlier characterization of Jerry as someone who could not simultaneously walk (actually, it was fart) and chew gum. Jerry stumbled in public a lot, and, being a bit taller and possibly a bit clumsier than other presidents, bumped his head on the doorway of Air Force One a lot. He was a terrible golfer.

These were the sort of attributes that, left to the mockery of Not Ready for Prime Time Player Chevy, could have reduced Jerry to a figure of public ridicule, dooming his presidency.

In truth, Jerry did experience a pretty rocky presidency. He was beset by raging inflation, energy shortages, two assassination attempts in a single month, plus several global flare-ups requiring American attention. Worst of all, he had to deal with the hangover from his predecessor's term, which decimated trust among the public, and which was complicated by Jerry's decision to grant Dick a full pardon. Many Americans thought the "fix was in," and that Jerry had cut a deal to pardon Dick in exchange for the presidency.

Today, that perception has changed. History has allowed us to get to know Jerry better. On one hand, it makes no sense that a guy that awkward and supposedly that dim was Machiavellian enough to get the better of a deal at that level.

But Jerry knew at the time that pardoning Dick—while it might anger people who wanted Dick's head on a pike—was essential if his administration was to be taken seriously in the world. With Dick on trial, Jerry's administration would be a footnote to its own term. By pulling the hook from the big fish's lip, he bought time and space for his own presidency.

To some extent, every leader needs to let the previous incumbent swim away. **Bad things happen when a prior boss hangs around**, whether in person or in memory:

- People say: "Well, that's not the way we did it under Barbara."
- People run to Barbara, down the hall, and ask her what she thinks of your approach.

- Barbara's six years of successful leadership make it hard for your leadership to make any initial penetration.

The Jack Nicholson movie *About Schmidt* contains a painful scene in which a newly retired Nicholson drops in on his replacement and is angered to discover the transition materials he had compiled for his successor stacked next to the company dumpster. The movie sided with Nicholson's feelings of rejection and rage. But an equally valid story is that of his young successor, who dreaded having his first foray into leadership handicapped by the recommendations of his predecessor.

A leader therefore has to create fresh space for the new regime. Sometimes it means pointedly rejecting past approaches. It is not that you are neurotic and self-absorbed and can't bear to be compared to your predecessor. (It had better not be.) It's that the efficient achievement of goals rather than the egos of leaders is what really matters, and **yoking the present to the past—even with the best intentions—invariably slows it down.**

It's tough sometimes, as Neil, a substitute American Studies teacher at a Connecticut college learned when he was hired to replace a teacher who passed away in mid-semester. Neil had never taught a full class before, and replacing this beloved figure was very hard.

"The students never really let me in. They felt they had already pledged allegiance to Miss Steffens, and it would be disloyal to hear my take on Nathaniel Hawthorne after hearing what Miss Steffens had to say. It was an impossible situation for me. When the semester ended, my evaluations were lousy, and I wasn't invited back."

Seven truths about effective team process:

1. Work is not the key process of a team. Deciding is.
2. The method it will use to make decisions is the most important decision the team will make.
3. Leaders risk losing their teams by imposing important decisions without first acquiring their members' consent.
4. Lines of communication don't work unless they are open.
5. The leader's job is to organize decisions into action steps.
6. Checkpoints are necessary for monitoring progress toward specific outcomes.
7. No team run with an iron hand ever came up with a new idea.

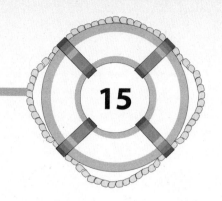

The Right (and Wrong)
Way to Make Up Your Mind

We have seen that getting your ducks in a row—setting up a plan of action—is a good thing. The next step is how people come to agree on that plan. But unfortunately we often make decisions without agreeing on a process for doing so.

The horrible truth is that most of the groups we belong to—work teams, investment groups, Boy Scout troops, ad hoc committees, the PTA, the president's cabinet in Washington, D.C.—make "illegal" decisions, decisions never legitimized by the agreement of the group. Since they don't have a set process by which to make decisions, the group winds up being dominated by the strongest, least shy personalities, who always get their way.

Your organization will pounce on a bad decision. But your team will resent a good decision made in an illegitimate way.

You need to get everyone on the same page, and that means settling on a decision-making method. The good news is, groups really have only seven ways they can make decisions. All are perfectly legitimate, on their own terms. They become illegitimate when team members disagree on what the decision-making method is.

Some members might be thinking, "Hey, you're the boss, you make the decision." You, in turn, are apt to be thinking, "We'll put it to a vote. They'll like that." Meanwhile, a third faction has already met in the cloakroom and decided the best way is to bring in a consultant to make the decision.

No one wants to rock the boat, and everybody is bending over backward being polite. It's chaos, and it wastes valuable time that you could be using to move the group toward desired outcomes.

Here are the seven basic decision-making methods. Decide which one you want to use as a default method for your group, and tell them what it is. You can always change it temporarily for special occasions, but stick with the default when possible.

1. **Car-pool**, also known as *consensus decision making,* works by soliciting everyone's input and getting everybody's OK. Nowadays, a million managers call themselves consensus-builders, because it makes them sound like nice guys, not tyrants. Upon reading a consensus decision, groups are still talking to one another, and that is good. But consensus exacts a price. By swallowing every idea, it niftily co-opts opposition. Consensus usually involves a ton of compromise and, in the end, a mediocre result. And it takes forever. What most people really want when they say they want consensus is really buy-in.

2. **Buy-in**, also known as *authority rule with discussion,* calls for the leader to make the decision, but only after consulting with team members and soliciting their opinions. After hearing enough to make an educated decision, the leader cuts off the discussion, makes the decision, then gets back to all team members to let them know how their input affected the decision. Buy-in provides clarity and accountability, and everyone feels they had their say.

3. **Top-down**, also known as *authority rule without discussion,* is where the leader just says, "This is how it's going to be." This is your basic autocracy. Here, a decision has been made way up in the organization and is rolling downhill. You can either catch hold of it as it rolls by or get run over. You had no input in making the decision, so don't fake it by asking for people's input. The dictatorial approach works well with administrative tasks and less well with political ones. Where the opinions of others matter, this approach undermines team spirit and commitment. Resentment and disagreement can lead to sabotage and group decay. (The variation we call **Mt. Sinai** cuts in when *you* are the autocrat issuing unquestionable decrees. Not recommended during the first hundred days. Trust is jeopardized when a group leader tries to steamroller group members into thinking that their opinions about the decision had an impact on the decision.)

4. **Vote-up**, also known as *majority rule,* is democracy—a simple vote in which the majority wins and the minority loses. It's quick, it's transparent, and it often quells dissent. Vote-up works when there's no time for a full-dress consensus process, or when the decision isn't so important that consensus is necessary, and when 100 percent member concurrence isn't essential for successful implementation. But it just as often creates an unhappy minority who may later try to subvert the decision.

5. **In-group**, or *minority rule,* forms a small subset of the larger group to go out and gather information and make a recommendation for a decision back to the larger group. When the expectation is that this recommendation must be accepted, the system doesn't make for broad commitment and buy-in. By not addressing everyone's concerns, even those of members with less expertise, the in-group approach can let important issues go unaddressed. Conflict and controversy may damage the group's effectiveness in the future.

6. **Center-strip**, also known as *averaging.* Averaging is consensus gone wild. You measure the spectrum of ideas and opt for the middle of the spectrum. In averaging, the middle is always the right answer. Usually no one is especially happy with the result, not even the moderates in the group, because it is a beast with many arms and legs.

7. **Outside-rule**, also known as *decision making by consultancy* or *expertocracy.* This is where you hire someone from the outside to tell you what you already know and charge you for their advice. Expertocracy is great for covering your anterior (CYA), because "No one ever got fired for hiring IBM." But: if *you're not* an expert, how do you know *your expert* is an expert?

How do you choose a default decision-making method? Choose based on the kinds of decisions your group will most often make. If your team is an implementing team, then rely on one of the more autocratic methods. They save time and promote clarity.

But if your team is involved in policy formation or any "political" consideration, you will want to slow down and make sure everyone's concerns are aired out.

Beware of fashion. Although business fads tilt to one or another of these approaches—consensus and democracy always "sound good" in a magazine article—there is really no right or wrong way to decide an issue.

The important thing is that everyone in the group understands, in advance, what decision-making method will be used. The worst thing a leader can do is spring a surprise on the group.

Get this assent in advance, and any decision you make will be made the right way.

Ten el-cheapo ways to motivate people:

1. **Celebrate the completion of outcomes**. A victory unnoted might as well not have happened.
2. **Keep outcomes short-term**. That way you have plenty of opportunities to celebrate.
3. **Show off for the big boss**. The more important the audience for a presentation, the more mileage the team will get from the success.
4. **Hand out mugs with the team logo all around**. That will keep reminding people where they belong.
5. **Give comp time**. Everyone likes comp time.
6. **Lunch together** (assuming you like to eat with each other).
7. **Bring in celebrities**. There's nothing like a show to acknowledge work well done.
8. **Hand out gift certificates**. It doesn't take much to make a great low-cost reward.
9. **Advance via retreat**. A weekend in the woods is nice.
10. When all else fails . . . **Krispy Kremes**.

Motivating People

Set aside all the flowery talk and high-mindedness, and leadership is something pretty gritty: **getting people to do what you want.**

When you look at it that way, leadership is a messy proposition. How do you succeed? Sometimes you have to scare people. Often, it's necessary to manipulate them—to present facts in such a way that compliance is the only logical response. Sometimes, when they need a little encouragement or approval, you give them a nice big smooch. Sometimes, all you do is explain the facts to them and walk away.

But how do you know when to do what? By getting to know the people on your team, and learning what makes different people tick. We'll talk about what different kinds of personalities need in a later chapter. For now, ponder the principle of motivation itself. We think it's flawed.

Motivation as it is practiced in most places arises from the notion that people in the workplace are like lab rats in a test box. Give a rat a pellet when it presses the proper lever, and you have motivated it to perform.

The problem is, most companies don't want to spend too much more to motivate workers than scientists do on rat pellets. So we have an endless succession of pep rallies, motivational meetings, and pump-em-up banners strung around the workplace. Experience teaches us that workers are motivated by all this stuff for a little while, then the motivation flags as they realize that there's precious little concrete incentive for them to perform, and that beyond the rah-rah atmosphere, they still lack the tools, or training, or systems (or worst of all, the product line) to be successful.

You can't even fool rats with such a scenario. You have to give them real rat pellets, or they stop pushing that little lever. People get wise almost as quickly. And beyond wise, they get cynical, and harder to reach with the next wave of marching bands and exhortations.

So, even if your organization is committed to this kind of P.T. Barnum motivation, you as a leader may want to think deeper about what makes people do things. It is as simple and as profound a question as *What do people want?*

What do they want? They want money, of course. The primary reason people are working for you is that they want to keep their bodies' cell walls from collapsing, and money for groceries and rent is a time-honored way to prevent this from happening. So cash performance bonuses are never out of fashion.

But you probably don't have gobs of cash to give away, so you'll have to look deeper. There are lots of rewards and incentives a leader can drop on workers that cost little or nothing, and that do make people feel good about themselves—and thus about their jobs.

Honor performance. One team we know rotates a stuffed skunk—the real thing, courtesy of a local taxidermist, not a plush toy—to the member who did something great that month. The idea is to give it to everyone at least one month per year. It's funny, but people appreciate it.

Invitations. The HR office at your company likely buys tickets to conferences and symposia on emerging business ideas. Why not get a handful of those tickets and distribute them to team members you want to reward?

Acknowledgments. It's easy with today's PC graphics to whip off attractive certificates when people do something really, really right. If your team is too hip for sincere certificates, give them joke certificates. ("Best Sales Month by an Admitted Introvert.")

Introductions. Take a team member with you when you meet with your superiors. It makes them feel connected to the hierarchy, it's a real compliment, and it lets your superiors see that you're helping develop leadership.

Parking. If your company still allocates reserved parking to managers, let people who do really well use your space for a day or a week. (Just remember to let Security know what you're up to so they don't hand out parking tickets to the lucky beneficiaries.)

Share credit. When good things happen, let the team take a bow. But be careful your reward ceremonies don't divide workers into winners and losers, or overstress individual achievement.

Paint the cubicle. Years ago, the Hawthorne experiments proved that people perform better when management fusses over them. Paint the office, move the furniture around, make them wear funny hats. Good or bad, the attention makes people feel connected, and they do better.

TLC. A good team is fueled by respect for one another's talents, effort, and individuality. Let teammates know their contributions are appreciated. The best way to do this is to *tell them.*

But we saved the best for last. More even than money, or perhaps tied in first place with money, **people want their work to mean something**.

As leader, your job is to hold the torch of the team goal high, so everyone can see it. But it is also to explain the team goal in terms that the team can respect, and respect themselves for pursuing. All work is meaningful and worthy of respect, even if you work in a pickle plant. You can be carrying a hod of bricks or you can be building a cathedral—the meaning is all in your perspective. But leaders must often fight a tide of pessimism and low worker self-esteem. Remember: even pickles have a purpose.

To overcome people's cynicism, you have to do two difficult and almost opposite things. You have to articulate the meaning of the work in ways they too can respect and buy in to.

("Our goal is to provide each customer who calls with an experience so positive they will want to call again, soon.")

But you also have to signal your empathy for their in-the-trenches humor. Lift up that lamp, but don't be high and mighty about it. If you can pull this off, there is a future for you.

William Edwards Deming, the man who taught quality to the Japanese, hated a lot of things that most leaders do. The thing that annoyed him the most was exhortation. Exhortation is when leaders become cheerleaders for the goal and seek to motivate workers through loud noises and banners.

Deming said that exhortation seeks to replace long-term rational processes and systems with the emotion of the moment, which never lasts. So exhortation doesn't work.

We agree with Mr. Deming. Most of the rah-rah motivation that goes on today achieves little, and it even has a negative effect when people see through the false enthusiasm to the problems inherent in the systems they work under.

But we can think of a major exception, and that is exhortation by deed. Clearly, **there is no better educational tool than a good example.** Showing workers that you mean business in your own habits is a powerful way of teaching them what you expect of them.

Ray, a new products team leader with an Internet company in Cupertino, did not intend to "send a message" his first day on the job when he brewed a fresh pot on the team's Mr. Coffee. "I was making coffee because I needed coffee," he says. But the team took it another way, recognizing him as a guy who wasn't above making coffee for everyone else. The previous team leader had team members make Starbucks runs just for him.

Estelle, new plant foreman at a Fairbanks cannery, decided after a week of business suits to wear blue jeans on the plant floor. Her message: "I know this is messy work, and I'm not above walking through it with you all." People got the message, and rallied around her just a bit as a result.

Different things motivate different people. The Quadrants of Success chart introduced in Chapter Four comes in handy here with a bit of updating, as shown in Exhibit 16.1.

For Doers, for example, the best motivation is being in charge of something, so give them more responsibilities and authority. For them, the joy of being not just in the chase but head dog is numero uno.

Exhibit 16.1. Goals in the Four Quadrants.

Thinkers being right	Doers being in charge
Socials being appreciated	Creatives being heard

For Creatives, it's new and challenging assignments requiring interaction with lots of interesting (or powerful) people. They are also motivated by deals and acknowledgment. Save them five dollars, give them a free T-shirt, and you have a new friend for life. Acknowledge their contributions, and they will light a perpetual flame in your honor.

For Socials it's the knowledge of appreciation. They need to be told how much they are valued by the company, and what's more important, by you personally. For these people, connections are everything, and a pat on the back works better than a barrel of glue.

For Thinkers the motivator is knowledge. Knowledge for them is ammunition in the war against imperfection. The chance to acquire new, rich information is like a trip to Disney World for them. The chance to associate with other smart people—sprinkles on the cake.

Five ways to effect change in the face of resistance:

1. People automatically fill in the blanks in their knowledge base with negative information—worst-case scenarios—for self-protection. Whenever left in the dark, people imagine monsters.
2. Counter this natural tendency with accurate information. Do not inflame people's automatic negative fears.
3. Change happens every day as a natural progression of living. The trick is to accept this stress and not overreact to it.
4. You have a choice: scaring your people into compliance with the change, or offering them a picture of a brighter future. One is push, the other is pull. When possible, choose *pull*.
5. Lay out a pathway to this brighter future so your people know you have a destination and a road map for getting them there.

Locating the
Levers of Change

A manager's job is to keep an existing machine running; a leader's job is to continually change the machine, always looking for a better way to meet team goals.

In an important sense, change is a leader's job. And that explains why it's so hard to be a good leader: because nearly everyone is scared of change.

People fear change because it takes them out of their comfort zone. It's a pleasant thing to have a steady machine that does all the work and requires little in the way of innovation, learning, or—horror of horrors—failure.

But today's workplace is the opposite of a steady machine. Products change, people come and go, new competitors arise, new technologies tap you on the shoulder and go Boo!

The drive to change—to make something cheaper, and better, and faster—keeps accelerating. So how, in this whirl of change, can leaders get leverage? By conducting a simple assessment and acting accordingly.

The first question a leader asks is: **How critical to the team's survival is the proposed change**?

Does the proposed change solve a major problem that the team faces? Or is it a challenge of a lesser order, either one that has been handed down by the organization as a whole (important, but survival is not at stake), or one that is worthwhile, but the team's survival is not at issue?

If the issue is clearly survival-critical, getting the team to make the change requires only that you explain it in terms of its gravity. Only very obtuse people, hearing that survival requires them to make adaptations, will sit on their hands. And these obtuse few can usually be moved to action by banging a pot over their heads.

But **change becomes more difficult as the issue becomes less acute**. When a team is told, "Yes, it would be a good thing if we restructure and reengineer key processes because some consultant from Boston says so," no one feels much motivation to move.

That's when the leader becomes a teacher. If the organization failed to describe the proposed change in terms that galvanize the team, then the job of galvanizing falls to you.

First, you must model your own belief in the change. No one will listen to you if you are not clearly convinced of the plan's merits.

Second, you must present the change to the team in a way that grips their attention. There are really only two things that reliably galvanize a team to change: *fear* and *conviction.* One is negative ("do this or risk losing your livelihood") and the other is positive ("this change is the pathway to greater profits and better job security, and it's interesting on its own terms").

Now you must sell the idea to the team, one person at a time, speaking to each in a way that mixes the negative and positive messages in just the right degree for that person.

Most people in the workplace are primarily motivated by negative emotions—"Do this or bad things will happen." There is nothing wrong with motivating with negativity, so long as you are telling the truth. If people don't get with the new system, the new product lines *will* fail, and they *will* lose their jobs. Sometimes people drift into denial, and they need to have this unpleasant reality spelled out for them.

Larry Bossidy, former chairman of AlliedSignal, describes what he calls the Burning Platform Syndrome. When a company is in trouble, it is like an offshore drilling platform that is on fire. Unless people leap to safety, and rapidly, the fire will destroy the company and kill its workers.

In a real fire, workers smell the smoke, hear the explosions, see the flames rising high above. But a business crisis produces no smoke, no explosions, and no flames. If stock price falls and the company becomes subject to takeover, there is no fire and no smoke, but the danger is every bit as great. Everything seems "normal," yet the leader desperately needs to get people to jump to a more survivable vessel. But how does a leader get people to do something that feels so wrong?

People who are motivated by positive things—perhaps 20 percent of the workforce, the 20 percent that you want to hug—will need little persuasion. They are largely self-motivating. They know the score. They know change is hard, but they also know it's doable. And because of the kind of people they are, they will be curious about creating a new way of working.

But the negative 80 percent will need all your persuasive power. With them you must become a skilled purveyor of practical fear, able to describe the dangers facing their team. You need to say to workers:

"Listen. You may not see the fire, but our company is in desperate trouble. We have to make important changes, and we need to make them right away. I can't guarantee that if we succeed, there will still be a job for you. But I can guarantee that if you do nothing, you will be out in the cold."

Nine ways to break an ice-jam in negotiations:

1. **Share information**. People struggling to find agreement have reason to be distrustful. Why not divulge information? It communicates the idea that mutual gain is a possibility—that I don't have to succeed by making you fail.
2. **Ask what's up**. Instead of trying to pry information from the other side, why not just ask for it? The chances of getting good information are better if you ask than if you don't ask.
3. **Pay attention**. When the other side is talking, it's tempting to sit back and plan your responses. Look for common interests to negotiate around. The information in their remarks provides many clues, which you will miss if you aren't listening carefully.
4. **Give something away**. Albert Einstein once said that nothing is ever yours until you give it away. If you want reciprocity, start by giving something away. It changes the tone and invites reciprocation.
5. **Make lots of offers**. Something will intrigue the other side and get you moving.
6. **Frost the cake**. Be on the lookout for "post-negotiation negotiations," bets and side deals that can extend and broaden the improved relationship.
7. **Barter**. People will often trade things, including information, that they would never sell.
8. **Praise cooperation** publicly and in print.
9. **Suggest rewards** for cooperative actions.

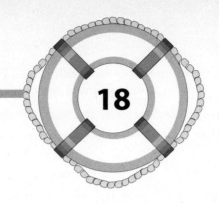

Learning to Negotiate

As an accidental leader, you probably won't be put in charge of formal negotiations—like for a labor contract, or a price—right away. Your organization should have other people, deeply skilled in the art of negotiating, to handle those tasks.

But in a more general sense, much of what you do is negotiation. Teaching, selling, explaining, motivating, and delegating are all tasks of negotiation—of bringing together two or more sides that are apart. Your job as leader is to move people along toward a goal. But **people are not cattle**. Disagreements arise, definitions of the goal mutate, and after a time the desire to do your bidding just because you are a nice boss begins to fade. . . .

Negotiating within your group is different from, say, selling a car in the classifieds, because you have to deal with everyone in the days and weeks that follow the negotiation. So you can't afford to negotiate brutally, or by withholding rightful information, or by playing two sides off against each other. Team negotiating is a narrow corridor, because you dare not behave in a way today that makes you untrustworthy hereafter.

As a team leader, you'll find that the other side—your teammates—is nearly the same side as yours, so negotiation will seldom break off because of mistrust or bad faith. But you must still bear in mind that other people have legitimate points of view, and you have to listen to them if you have any hope of your point of view being heard.

What follows are tips on how to negotiate, inspired in part by the teachings of some of the top negotiating authorities, William Ury and Roger Fisher, authors of the classic *Getting to Yes*. They stress that the secret to successful negotiating is to sit down at the table ready to do some fresh thinking, thinking that is empathic to the needs and wants of the other side.

First, depersonalize the debate.

The biggest problem people have in coming to an agreement is that they get too emotional about winning, or more precisely, about not losing. Suspicions and fears swirl around the process, and a lot is often at stake, and it is easy to start demonizing the other side. Once you do that, and you've decided the other side is no longer a sensible, rational person (like yourself!), any chance for a result satisfactory to both sides is gone. The solution is to focus on the problem at hand instead of the people trying to solve it. If you're prone to play the blame game, this will be very difficult.

One approach we like is to take turns describing the problem until each side agrees with the description provided by the

other. Instead of sitting on opposite sides of a table, consider sitting on one side of a blackboard, and working out
the problem together. Instead of battling one another, like
two dogs over one bone, work together to see if there is a
better way.

"When I came aboard we already had an all-out turf war
blossoming between engineering and production at our Clarks-
ville facility," said Turley, head of sales engineering for a
Mississippi-based pipe manufacturer. People on the factory
floor thought we were a bunch of dilettantes flipping specs
to them on paper airplanes. And we thought they were trying
to set some sort of record for foot-dragging. Schedules were
backed way up. When the production chief asked me to lunch,
I thought, 'Oh, no, he's gonna take out the new guy.' But the
first thing he said after we sat down was, 'Tell me, what can we
do on our end to get parts out the door faster?' We wound up
talking for three hours. I think it was the best talk I ever had."

Second, set aside demands and focus on what's good.

If two sides slap mutually canceling sets of ultimatums on
the table, what chance do they have of coming to agreement?
Too much certainty spells the death of negotiation. Instead
of a narrow, rigid demand, go to the table aware of the length
and breadth of all that you need. You are always likely to en-
counter "position opposition." But in the broader scheme of
things, both sides often share important interests. The skilled
negotiator is on the lookout for this kind of common ground.

"Our firm was in trouble," said Stan, newly named managing
partner for a twenty-member law firm in Ottawa, "and it was
my job to go to each partner and ask if they could kick in
another four billable hours per week. It was a lot to ask, but

we were in dire straits. Everyone agreed, except Sheila, a partner in the litigation group. She just stonewalled and said 'No way.' I was authorized to tear her contract up, and she wasn't giving me much reason not to. Before I did that, I asked her why she couldn't do what every other partner could. 'I'd like to help the firm,' she said. 'But I'm divorced and I've got a five-year-old boy who gets severe asthma attacks, and I'm already spending too much time away from him.' Well, that changed everything. We exempted Sheila from the new requirement, and life went on."

Third, be creative.

Many negotiations bog down in compromise, the end product of which neither side recognizes or claims. The problem with compromise is that it assumes a zero-sum game, a pie that has to be cut up into X number of pieces—the only question being, how many slices. But **creative negotiators try to enlarge the pie.** They've come up with all sorts of ways to brainstorm new options that deliver solid value to both sides. For example, A negotiation can be seasoned with a series of if-then agreements. "If your group meets X level of production, we agree to pay Y level of bonus." The beauty of this sort of bet is that it makes good things possible for both sides without costing either side anything at the outset.

A Roanoke naval base supply department competed for business with a similar department in Naples, Italy. For years both teams underbid one another for overnight shipment business throughout the U.S. armed forces—a form of brutal price negotiation. At Roanoke, the new captain made a bet with the supply captain in Naples, offering a kind of collusion that governmental entities can engage in and that businesses can't. "You take the European and Atlantic business, we'll take Asia and the Pacific." And here's the creative part: If either department experienced reduced sales after two quarters, they would reapportion the globe with markets in Africa and Antarctica providing the balance.

Finally, strive to keep your negotiating lucid.

You've surely taken part in auctions, which are a kind of rapid-fire price negotiation. Auctions are driven first by greed (hoping to get something for nothing), then by fear (uh oh, the price is starting to climb), and finally by a kind of suicidal vengefulness ("So what if I lose—I'm going to make that buzzard's victory unbearable").

The fact is, people often not only negotiate dumb, they negotiate crazy. Negotiating rationally is the best avenue open to anyone, but it is not easy to change negotiating styles and habits. The trick is to identify the kinds of mistakes you systematically make and guard against ever making them again.

Is it better to be a tough negotiator or a cream puff? Neither. Being too pliant, too eager to please, relinquishes too much of the bargaining zone. Yet the tough negotiator—the one with the belt notches for every victory extracted at the team's expense—soon discovers no one wants to bargain anymore. The game's over, and probably the chance at leadership as well.

Four kinds of people, and how to work with each:

1. **Doers**, people who themselves wish to be leaders, to be in charge of something. These are people who need the least direction, because they are already motivated by nature to expend great effort to achieve things.
2. **Thinkers**, those who are gifted in reason and able to achieve deep understanding of issues and facts. For these people, the most important thing is to be right.
3. **Socials**, people who like working with other people. They derive greatest satisfaction from communicating and relating to other people.
4. **Creatives**, people who easily generate new ideas and fresh perspectives. Their great need is to get stuff out of themselves.

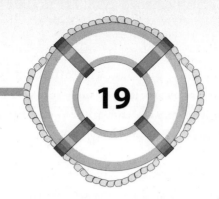

Dealing with Other People

So what, finally, is leadership? As we said in Chapter Sixteen, it's the gritty business of *getting people to do what you want them to do.* And you do that by scaring or them or by inspiring them. What it boils down to is messy but simple:

You have to know when to scare, and when to inspire.

The way to know when is by getting to know the people under your command. No two people on your team will be quite alike. But broadly, we can say that each occupies a spot on a continuum, stretching from easy-to-lead to difficult-to-lead.

In the days before cross-functional teams, it was possible to spend one's entire career surrounded by people who did the same kind of work you did. If you were an actuary, chances are you spent your days with other actuaries, calculating insurance probabilities. It was likely you communicated on a reliably high level with the other team members, because you all thought the same way.

That's gone in today's team environment. While many kinds of organizations still have people within functions working alongside one another, most organizations are more integrated. Even in a restaurant there are huge cultural and personality differences between the hospitality crew, the wait staff, the bar staff, the kitchen help, and the chef. Not to mention the customers. And you have to learn to get along and get things done with all these types of people.

Practically speaking, people have four distinct personality types: **Doers, Thinkers, Socials, and Creatives.** Each of us has a little of all four of these elements, but most of us are dominant in one of the four. That area is our "home base," and it determines most of our responses in life. Thus a Doer can also be a creative person, or a Social may also have a knack for analysis. But when the chips are down, the Doer reverts to being a taskmaster and the Social to being a people person.

The relevance of all this is that as a leader, you have the best chance of convincing your people to follow if you understand what kind of people they are, and adapt your appeal accordingly.

What makes a Doer happy? Opportunities to demonstrate forcefulness and energy. This is what we call a gung-ho person. Tap into one or more Doers under you and you will have a pool of powerful enforcers to draw on. They understand command, and they do not require that you explain things six ways. The downside with Doers is that ultimately they will want to replace you, or to go somewhere else where they can be in charge. It is in their blood to be that way. If you can live with that tension, you're likely to succeed with your Doers.

Thinkers are a very different story. Thinkers are perfectionists, and their great fear is of making a mistake. As such they can be extremely resistant to change, coming up with countless rationales for not moving forward. How does a leader overcome analytical resistance? By respecting the Thinker's legitimate fears and providing counterevidence supporting the proposed change. Show that you respect their painstaking methods. Do not make an emotional appeal to a Thinker—if you do, all is lost. Consider creating a special role for the Thinker, that of measuring the progress of the new change.

Socials are terrific coordinators and natural diplomats, because their province is people. As a result they tend to be suspicious of change "on paper" because, to them, the best and most natural change is what people move intuitively toward. They are evolutionists, not revolutionists. The problem is that time is short, and revolution is what is called for. The way to get Socials moving in your direction is by being nice to them. They need TLC and a sense that you care about them as people. Give them that, and they will repay you with fierce loyalty.

The Creatives are the artists in your midst. Creatives are not egomaniacs exactly, but they are self-involved in ways the other types are not. They enjoy stimulation above all else— including consistency, details, and sometimes logic. They can be powerful additions to a team, but they must be dealt with on their own terms. They must know that you appreciate their lively turn of mind, and that you don't see them as cogs but as living, passionate persons. They appreciate openness, but they are not immune to flattery. Treat them as what they are: ever-bubbling fonts of ideas, some very good, and some— well, some others. Respect their inner spark, and you will own their souls.

This may seem more psychological than practical to you at first, because of the terms and categories. But move beyond that feeling, because understanding differing orientations is one important key to successful leadership.

"I learned how to lead from my mom," says Trisha, a Methodist minister in Spokane. "She was an empathic person who could also teach empathy. When I was little she used to tell me, 'Pay attention to other people, and try to think what things seem like to them.' What you will find is that 99.99 percent of everybody is trying to do good work, but we misfire a lot when we communicate with one another. You have to work at it, but what it really comes down to is realizing that **the person sitting across from you is as real as you are**. Once you admit that, anything is possible."

Once you learn to speak to people in ways they are able to really *hear,* a whisper will get heard. Until you learn to speak that way, you might as well be shouting into a hurricane.

Three ways to give people information so it is real to them:

1. Verbally. (Tell them face to face.)
2. In writing. (Tell them on paper or via e-mail.)
3. Kinesthetically. (Let them learn by doing, as they like to work through the process.)

Which way is best? Depends. Try being *bi-modal* (provide info two ways at once). Say, call them on the phone and follow up with an e-mail note, or vice versa.

Remember to give feedback based on the receiver's personality:

- If someone is a **Doer**, feedback needs to be direct, specific, brief, and with new outcomes and expectations. Bullet points are good.
- With a **Creative**, you need to support your target's ability to generate ideas and provide lots of options for future outcomes.
- For a **Social**, you must make sure to not bruise that fragile ego. Be gentle and kind—but hold firm to expected outcomes.
- For a **Thinker**, you need to have specific behaviors listed as examples, with lots of documentation.

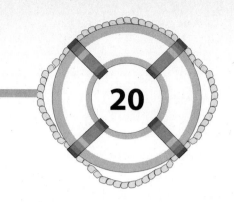

How to Give Feedback

I worked for the firm for nineteen months, and no one ever said boo to me. There were times I wasn't sure if I was doing a good job or a bad one, but no one ever complained or suggested a better way to me. Then one day, I got a pink slip—unsigned, in the mail. It was the most cowardly thing I ever saw in my life."

One of the hardest tasks for accidental leaders is giving people feedback. "Giving people feedback" is a neutral description for something decidedly un-neutral—telling people how they could be doing their jobs better. And because it is a loaded area, with a high potential for ticking people off and alienating them just when you need them to be "on your side," lots of leaders get confused and inept.

Why is giving feedback hard for us? Probably because people think it has to be done very cleverly—delicately—so as not to offend anyone. And most of us are not clever, so we despair.

And procrastinate. And when push finally comes to shove, and we sit down with the person in question, we criticize crappily.

How do we do that? Let us list the ways.

We do it *too formally*. We invite the other person in to the boss's office. We sit on opposite sides of a desk. We refer to reports for information, sometimes hiding behind the pages. Six-month evaluations may be good for record keeping, but a better way to keep people on point is to evaluate them every single day, with attention, instruction, availability, and acknowledgment of a job well done. Fix a problem informally, and it need never appear in someone's file.

We *wait* too long. "Harold, it's come to our attention you've been taking two-hour naps every afternoon since 1994." The time to step in and advise is early, before something becomes a bad habit, and before you become irritated with the behavior's deep-seatedness. Also, workers have every right to protest. They would have been happy to make the change earlier—if someone had only asked. Delaying puts an unnecessary black mark on their record.

We keep it *one-way*. Feedback is properly described as a loop. You tell them something, they tell you something, and so on. The process belongs to both of you. If it's just you informing a worker—much less, a teammate—that they have failed, doesn't that tell you something about the team?

We *apologize*. We mince about. There is no way to tell someone an unpleasant truth and come out of it more popular than you went in. The proper and honest thing to do is say it directly: "Mary Ann, I'm concerned about the quality of your follow-up work. Several times I've had customers complain, and I want to fix the problem right now, before it becomes a *real* problem." They may not like you more. They may emerge from the talk bruised and a little scared. But they will know what is expected of them. Clarity will help them survive, whereas friendly gobbledygook could lead them to destruction.

We *beat around the bush*. We say nineteen positive nice things in order to soften the blow of the twentieth item, which is negative. In all things strive for clarity. A good meeting has a single purpose. "Jack, I want to talk to you about your absence last week."

We don't think it's feedback *unless it's negative*. We're not saying to camouflage the one negative observation behind nineteen compliments. But why is it we only call workers in to see us when we have bad news? Invite them in when you notice something great. What a simple message to communicate: we value your positive contributions, and we want to encourage you to keep trying.

We go in with *too much certainty*. "Dave, you've not been attentive in your work." Instead, try: "Dave, I'm concerned that you aren't giving your work your full attention. You make a lot of funny remarks at team meetings, but I'm not sure you're kicking in with the right amount of effort. Do you agree with that assessment?"

We put it all on *the other person*. Maybe Esther isn't meeting quota for reasons that Esther has little control over. Maybe you think Esther has been properly trained, but she hasn't. Maybe there's something you can do that will help Esther perform.

We criticize, but we are vague about *future action*. Feedback must be action-oriented or it is just blather. State a desired outcome, and slap a schedule on it. Then, if the teammate misses the outcome by the date agreed upon, who can complain about the consequences?

If it helps, don't think of evaluation as a dreaded task, like handing out report cards. See it as part of a logical continuum. A leader's job, after all, is to communicate the mission. Usually you do that with the whole group. With feedback, you're doing the same thing with people on a one-to-one basis. Communicating the mission, with specific reference to performance—that's all feedback is.

So don't fear it. It's not your enemy. In fact, it's your quality check, to make sure everyone is clear on the leadership you've been providing.

But we've run into three special categories of people who may require special consideration. We're going to use shorthand to label them: *brats, jerks,* and *demons.* These categories may sound flippant, but you will be glad you have them when you have to assess people you just can't accommodate on your team.

Brats are people who just don't seem able to carry a grown adult's load. They can be young, or they can be old. But they have a defect in their nature. Mature people have what is called an "internal locus of control"—they see themselves as primary actors in their lives and careers. Immature people, on the other hand, have an "external locus of control"—they see themselves as spinning in a blender, the victims of forces beyond their control.

In the workplace, brats may be fair workers, but they are awful team members because they are hard-pressed to step forward with ideas, and disinclined to take the risks associated with innovation. Big corporations have a history of taking ordinarily capable people and turning them into brats through policies and procedures that strip them of accountability. We call this the environment of entitlement—where workers can perform or gather wool, and they get paid either way.

Brattism in the news: A state-run university in the southwestern United States discovered that for the past eleven years, more than forty workers in the plant services department were working four days a week for five days' pay. This unwritten and unmeasured practice continued under four consecutive administrators, each one afraid to withdraw a valued perk. The cost in squandered productivity was staggering: an estimated $18 million of taxpayers' money. When the university ordered the practice discontinued, workers sued the university for breach of contract!

The correct response to brattism, whether it is innate to the individual or created by a pampering corporate culture, is—you saw it coming—to lower the boom on the brat. If your organization does not have a riot act, now is the time to draft one, and to read it loud and clearly to these people—*swim or sink.*

But be forewarned: many of these people won't get it even when you write it in the snow for them. Their feelings of helplessness, of being on the receiving end of everything, are too deeply ingrained. Sadly for them, they will have to learn to change the hard way, by finding a new job.

Jerks are people who are unable to see the effect they have on others. A more clinical way to describe them is "socially impoverished." Ordinarily, we would not lose sleep over jerks. But many jerks are very talented. Indeed, it seems to be their curse to have an imbalance of gifts: to be very good at non-people matters but astonishingly inept with people. They can be cruel, callous, stupid, or just monumentally insensitive. Famous jerks include Steve Jobs, Miles Davis, and Sharon Stone. But many more are jerks in relative anonymity.

A celebrated New York magazine editor agreed to create a new magazine with a $40 million start-up bankroll. But the publisher learned to his dismay that turnover at the Fifth Avenue HQ was running 25 percent per month. The editor was too demanding, too critical, and too crazy for even ambitious journalists to be around for very long. The publisher's solution: retain the woman's glamour assets by promoting her to executive editor and putting her in charge of media appearances—with only indirect management of the magazine's content.

So the leader with a jerk on the team has a big problem: how to capture the brilliance without inhaling the exhaust. Forget sensitivity training. Jerks don't take well to it.

First, acknowledge the truth, that this person can't help behaving in a beastly fashion. Perhaps you can sit your jerk down for a heart-to-heart talk and go over the most egregious behavior and the ways it screws things up. But you are not going to be able to tame this rude, snorting creature and get anything else done.

Second, create a playpen. Jerks who are geniuses need their own space and a special relationship to the rest of the team. Some leaders draw a dotted line and set the jerk up as a resource to the rest—but a resource like a fire-axe, one you don't turn to except in dire emergencies. Or you can name the jerk to a one-person team, or even let the jerk work from home, phone in the genius, and save a parking space for someone else.

Demons are outright sociopaths. Brats and jerks you can work around. Demons, you can't. A demon is constitutionally unable to work with other people, and is quite likely to endanger team projects.

Demons include people who have been brutalized into pathology; people who have abused themselves with addictions and obsessions until they can no longer function healthily; angry people who have a score to settle and don't mind settling it with you; and sadists, who enjoy inflicting pain and causing trouble.

Anoushka was the only child of a financial services entrepreneur in New Delhi. Her father wanted to bring her up in his company, and started her out as assistant director of marketing and communications. She knew nothing about the business and wasn't interested in learning about it. Her focus was on intimidating workers and vendors. She was just plain mean. A special triumph for her was to have work done, and then make the contractor eat the costs. She thrived on this kind of behavior for four years until her reputation reached the nostrils of her father, who, sensing her poisonous impact on his business network, granted her every ambitious executive's dream—early retirement.

It doesn't matter if a demon is a genius. It doesn't matter if the demon has the manners of an angel. It doesn't matter if a demon has a recipe for cold fusion in a desk drawer. Demons are fatal news to whatever organization will have them. And once you have identified a person as being this toxic, your only choice is to scrub them totally out of your organization.

Three ways to make empowerment work—and make your team bless you:

1. Don't expect your people to read your mind.
2. Communicate to workers exactly what they are empowered to do, and where their empowerment ends.
3. Limit their power by a dollar amount. Anything over that amount, they need to ask permission.

Set Limits to Freedom

One of the more confusing fads rolled out in the 1990s was *empowerment*. Empowerment was an offshoot of the self-managing aspect of teams and the new science of customer satisfaction. Basically, it said to workers: *Do whatever you have to do to make customers happy.*

Empowerment made a lot of customers happy, but it made workers nervous because few had been trained to make decisions that could cost their organizations money. It was not uncommon for workers to make decisions that cost their companies far more than the companies intended to spend.

As new business models were rolled out, organizations began to lose confidence in empowerment. Things largely returned to the bad old days when workers had no authority to do anything to satisfy customers or make improvements to the workplace.

It is deeply depressing to a team to go to all the trouble of learning how to solve a problem only to be paralyzed and unable to implement that solution because it doesn't know if it's allowed to do so. Or worse, to turn around and implement what it knows is a wrong (but defensible) solution because it doesn't think management will go for the right (but ambitious) one.

What was supposed to be such a good idea, people doing the right thing on their own recognizance, deteriorated into a high-stakes guessing game, with neither workers nor leaders sure what was going down. **Empowerment ground to a halt.**

Teams and managers today need some sort of arbitration, so the teams can do things to advance their cause without wreaking havoc on the larger organization's sense of control.

What shape might that arbitration take? Instead of broadly empowering people to do "whatever," think in terms of *boundary management*. Boundary management is the process of setting limits to power, defining what the power is, who has it, where it starts, and where it ends.

Instead of telling workers, "Do whatever you think seems right and we'll probably back you up on it"—a prescription for dread—inform workers what their decision-making limits are:

- *You have the power* to adjust bills up to $100 on your own, on the spot, to make amends for customer dissatisfaction. Over $100, you ask permission.
- *You have the power* to delay delivery of a product for one week on your own, to make sure it is done right. Longer than that, you ask permission.

- *You have the power* to allocate purchasing costs up to 5 percent of the total to improve the order (enlarging type size on a print order, for instance) without getting permission. Above 5 percent, you get permission.

Empowerment is a good idea. It puts authority in workers' hands—those who are closest to customers and processes—to do good things. But to keep it from tipping into abuse, a regimen of boundary management is necessary.

Five rules for dealing with conflict:

1. **Encourage people to express their opinions**. Being polite doesn't put any ideas on the table.
2. **Focus on the mission when disagreements arise**. Don't be distracted by the people.
3. **Warn people to avoid aggressive behavior**. (Or you'll beat the crap out of them.)
4. **Issue fines when people launch attacks on someone they disagree with**. Cash fines, payable immediately.
5. **Collect people's opinions individually in potentially difficult situations**. Summarize them in writing and feed back the summary to the whole group.

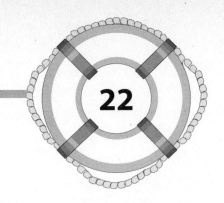

The Importance of Being Frank

One of the biggest misconceptions is that leading means keeping the peace, that it means keeping disagreements from cropping up among the people you lead.

It's not hard to see where this idea comes from. Disagreements make a team seem un-unified, and can conceivably reflect on a leader's ability to maintain order. So the "good" leader steps in and smoothes disagreements over before they become destructive.

Here's where we have some contrarian advice for you: **Don't be so good**. And don't be afraid of conflict.

Stop and ask yourself, Why do we have teams in the first place? Why is it better to have multiple heads solve problems rather than one single head?

The answer is that multiple heads know more things, and can create a broader diversity of possible solutions, than a single head can.

So how does a team get its multiple heads thinking effectively together? It's a four-stage deal.

Teams pass through four stages as they develop strength, and your team has to go through all four if it wants to be effective:

- **Forming**. Coming together and figuring out what your mission is and what the rules of engagement will be.
- **Norming**. The awkward "polite" stage where everyone bends over backward to get along.
- **Storming**. The most important stage, where you find ways to disagree without destroying the group. It can be arduous, and it can be threatening to your leadership, because you will require people to rise up and tell you the truth. But unless you go through this phase, your team will never be worth a damn, because it will be too chicken-hearted to speak its own wisdom.
- **Performing**. The stage of competence, where the team settles down from its struggles and does its best work. It can be a rut if you sidestep the lessons of storming. Or it can be a stone groove, if you harness the power of different skill-sets and opinions and put them to work.

So at some point you *want* disagreement. And, up to a point, you want people to feel free to argue their side. When you author an idea, you put your entire person behind it, so argument is often passionate.

A team that strives for peace among its members as a #1 criterion will get peace, but at a cost—stifled expression. Everyone will be so polite to everyone else that the quality of thinking and doing is not likely to be very high.

A team that can't argue is like a doorknob, only minus the utility. And "nice guy" managers, determined to keep group processes on an amiable, nonthreatening level, can hamper a team's ability to be honest, creative, and collaborative.

"I was a preacher's kid," said Gloria, group leader for a large Houston law firm. "It was embedded in me that you have to keep people smiling. 'Never a discouraging word,' and all that. I sensed it was a phony way to maintain control, and my team called me on it. 'How are we going to get anywhere unless we speak our minds?' was how one partner put it. I didn't have a good answer.

"If I was to stay in charge and credible to my group, I had to change my whole tolerance level for conflict. My husband had me watch Sunday morning political programs, like the McLaughlin Group, to prove it was OK to let people yell a bit. I still think those programs are abusive, but watching helped me relax to the idea of people duking it out. I like our meetings now. We have 'frank exchanges,' just like diplomats in the news. But it's good. People speak their minds, then we decide, and we rally behind the group's decision."

Disagreement and conflict only become bad when one of two things happens: they hang a team up, or they take a sick turn and become really nasty.

That's what the leader is for, however. You don't let the issue hang up. You remind people of the need to act on the mission. If necessary, you make the decision yourself, then sell it to the team. They did their part, surfacing the pros and cons. Now you do your part, and set the plan in motion.

We all fear nasty behavior, but if you keep the mission prominent in people's minds, they should be able to argue their points without getting personal. Some people may not have the social skills to keep these elements separate. As leader, you step in and remind people that they're encouraged to be vocal, but not abusive. **Clean shots, not cheap shots**!

Just because you permit people to speak their minds doesn't mean the loudest team members should be allowed to dominate. It is natural for some members to be extroverted and others to be more inward. Let the more ebullient members have their fun, but at some point rein them in and require that every team member have input into a decision.

You can be absolutely direct with the big mouths about this. "That's great, Dave. But we want to get everyone's opinion here. Julia?"

Theo, at a British Columbia engineering firm, recalls how one team member continually crossed the line of propriety:

"We had this one guy, Riley, who seemed to get satisfaction from reminding people how their previous ideas had failed. When he did this, it was a real conversation-killer. He hurt people, and angered them, and then the argument was no longer about the problem at hand, it was protecting yourself from Riley, or getting back at him.

"I sat Riley down and asked where the heck he got off dissing his teammates. He said it was just the way he was, and he'd been talking that way for years. In the old days there were people who talked to him that way, and he picked it up out of self-defense.

"'Well,' I told him, 'Those days are gone. Disagree on substance, but when you attack people's competence and even their good intentions, you're a danger to the team.'

"I'd like to say Riley got the message and was a sweetheart after that, but he wasn't. Six weeks later, we dropped him from the team."

Five broad characterizations of the working generations:

1. **Traditionalists** like structure and hierarchy.
2. **Boomers** rebel against Traditionalists, so they are suspicious of structure and hierarchy, and intrigued by collaboration.
3. **N-gens**, the next half-generation (between age thirty-six and forty-five these days) are the first truly collaborative culture. They are mad at Boomers for being the dominant demo-bubble.
4. **Gen-X** (twenty-six to thirty-five) like technology, and hark back to Traditionalists in that they respect hierarchy.
5. **Gen-Z** (sixteen to twenty-five) are reacting against Gen-X and looking for collaborative solutions to problems.

Note how each demographic blip defines itself in opposition to the group that preceded it. . . .

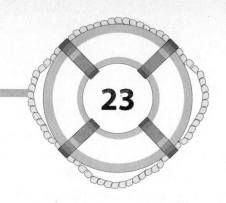

Bridging the Age Gap

We've talked about the difficulties of dealing with different types of personalities—Thinkers, Doers, Creatives, and the like. But leaders experience additional pitfalls dealing with people who are different from them in other ways—gender, background, and age.

A great deal has been made about the need to develop and appreciate greater diversity in the workforce, and to protect women and members of various minority groups from discrimination. Unless you are willing to sell only to some subset—say, middle-aged white men wearing ties—you'd be well advised to hire people from the full spectrum. You need their different perspectives to succeed and grow.

But you also need to learn how to deal with people who are not cookie-cutter copies of yourself. Different orientations mean different understandings. Hopefully, after all the suffering and struggle by disenfranchised peoples over the last fifty years, you do not need a great deal of persuading on this score.

The big problem we are seeing today is in the area of age, and we would not call it discrimination so much as **miscomprehension**. The problem is not between middle-aged and senior-aged workers, but between middle-aged Baby Boomers and the subgenerations coming up behind them, sometimes called Generations X and N.

How are the generations different, and how might you treat people of different generations differently?

What follows are generalizations—surely not true in every case. But they are true enough, often enough, that you ignore them at your peril. Ages given are for the year 2003.

- **Traditionalists** (roughly fifty-seven years old and up) prefer traditional, hierarchic structures, and are most likely to respect leaders who occupy a superior position and title. Hey, they saw a world war won that way.
- **Boomers** (roughly forty-six to fifty-six years old) are more likely to favor a shared leadership model, with non-traditional structures. They are more of a meritocracy, preferring leaders who prove their skills, not just give orders because of their position. Perhaps because of the Vietnam experience, they tend to be uncomfortable with the U.S. role as sole global superpower.
- **N-gens**, or the "Net Generation," (roughly thirty-six to forty-five years old) are the first truly collaborative culture. They dress casually, and they embrace information technology without reservation. N-gens believe in *shared leadership,* and like Boomers are suspicious of traditional leadership. They want to follow the person with the best ideas at

a given time, not necessarily the person with the title on the door.

- **Gen-X** (roughly twenty-six to thirty-five years old) are technology dependent, and they have moved back to traditional hierarchy. Many are wearing suits to work. They typically desire strong leader figures to follow—people whose authority is rooted in position and title. Unlike the Boomers, they are confident about America's role as superpower.
- **Gen-Z** (roughly sixteen to twenty-five years old) are swinging back in the direction of collaboration. They look for strong leadership, wherever it may be, and they are very worried about image—their own image, and that of their country. They value creativity and look to technology to solve world problems.

The upshot of all these generations and subgenerations is mistrust and suspicion.

What can you do with these generalizations? **Not a whole heck of a lot**, stereotypes being what they are. Good leaders treat individuals as individuals, not as members of defined groups.

But it is useful to note that a sense of "generation" is very important to each of these groups. We form thirty friendships within our generation before we form one outside it. (It's why old people are often lonely: their cohort is dying.) We treasure and find comfort in our generation's shared experiences and outlook.

It is not easy for a leader of one generation to win over another generation, particularly a younger one, by charm or charisma alone. What's cool to one era is the opposite of cool to the one that follows. The entire function of generational cultures is to exclude older or younger people, to protect the people in that age group.

We have seen Boomer managers bomb out utterly by adopting what they imagined was hip jargon with twenty-year-olds, like using the phrase "totally tubular," unaware that the boat has sailed on that expression. You might as well try to win over World War II veterans with the word "gnarly" or kindergartners with "23 skidoo."

What does communicate across the generations? Sincerity, clarity, standard English, and an occasional glint of self-deprecation. Interestingly, modesty seems never to go out of style.

So pay attention to this idea. Find out from individual team members what they need from you as a leader. Some, according to their preferred style, will want more supervision, direction, or collaboration. Some will want less.

At minimum, make a note to yourself that the things that motivate one worker demographic do not necessarily motivate another.

Four of the worst and six of the best ways to communicate bad news:

Don't . . .

1. **Blow your top**. Anger undermines your authority and underscores your immaturity.
2. **Blame**. Personalizing the difficulty only makes it harder to discuss.
3. **Be afraid to describe negative consequences**. Don't soften the blow with niceties.
4. **Resort to the silent treatment**. Shutting down communication merely emphasizes that you can't communicate.

Do . . .

1. **Be specific**. Use facts that the other person will agree are true. You don't want to appear to be acting out of general impressions or personal opinion.
2. **Be real**. Maintain perspective over the underperformance. Don't be a drama queen.
3. **Bring in other people**. Talk to others, and collect their opinions, to show that the negativity isn't something personal.
4. **Be candid**. Communicate increasingly harsh consequences for noncompliance.
5. **Solve the problem**. Before you fire someone, see if you can solve the problem in a less drastic way. Brainstorm. Coming up with workable solutions is what leaders are supposed to do.
6. **Act**. Once all solutions have been vetted, drop the hammer. It's not fair to leave the other person hanging for months.

24

How to
Discipline and Fire

Here's a common question: How do you decide you can't carry an employee or teammate any further?

We become leaders for reasons of success, not because we hanker for the power of life and death over one another's careers.

So naturally, the prospect of giving up on another human being goes against the grain. Firing someone or laying them off is really an act of despair—of their ability to adapt, and of your own ability to lead the change.

But it still has to be done sometimes, so here are some guidelines.

Having someone work for you is governed by something called the employment-at-will doctrine. It means that, in most cases, **an employer can fire an employee for any reason or for no reason at all.**

There are exceptions, however. First, you may never fire someone for reasons that discriminate against legally protected classes of people. You know the list: race, color, religion, sex, and national origin. And to be on the safe side, add less protected classes such as age, lifestyle, and political affiliation to that list. Fire someone for one of these reasons, and you deserve whatever happens to you.

Second, you can't fire someone for reasons that break other laws. You can't fire whistle-blowers, for instance, or people who are involved with unions, or people who file for worker's compensation.

Third, you can't be a predator. You can't ask an employee out on a date and then issue a pink slip for refusing, or for not capitulating. This is another reason never to get personally involved with people in your work group. Even if you have proper reasons to discipline them, they can throw this back at you, and people will take note.

The thing is, if you can't prove that you fired someone for a proper reason, it may look like you fired them for discriminatory reasons. So by all means, keep good records of problems you are having with workers.

Another good idea is to establish a warning policy, so people know if they are on the bubble to termination. **Getting fired or laid off should never come as a surprise.** People whose performance has been subpar should be aware of that—and aware of the consequences if they don't get it together.

If a company or a business unit is in trouble, and layoffs are in order, people should not be sheltered from these business realities. The best companies link everything to team success—compensation, recognition, and rewards. But sometimes things happen that have nothing to do with the caliber of work performed, or even the profitability of a team's work. For instance, the company can make a strategic decision that takes it in a different direction, leaving an effective and hardworking team high, dry, and unnecessary.

Your job as the bearer of bad news is to be direct, honest, and supportive. Inform people what the problem is. Remind them of reminders you have already issued. Where appropriate, point them in a direction that is better suited to their abilities.

Give people bad news early in the day, and early in the week. Avoid Christmas Eve.

Be ready. If you are sure of your action, have all the paperwork on hand explaining severance pay, benefits, and unused vacation. On the other hand, if you're not sure and just need to confront the person, better not have these things ready.

Bring backup. Sometimes it's a good idea to have someone else on hand, like someone from human resources. Having another person there keeps the scene from devolving into personalities. And workers often ask questions you didn't anticipate.

Keep it on the QT. Discipline and termination are extremely private matters. Assure the worker that nothing said in the room leaves the room.

Keep it short if not sweet. This meeting should last no more than ten minutes. Longer than that, and it becomes a desperate negotiation.

Try to learn something yourself. A firing is a failure, and we try to learn from failures. Is there anything the employee can tell you to shed light on the failure?

Finally, say you are sorry things didn't work out, and that you take responsibility for your part in the failure. Avoid saying, "I know what you're going through," even if you've been on the receiving end yourself. This meeting is not about you.

Let the other person speak. You are handing down a sentence. They deserve some choice last words. If it gets ugly, repeat that you are very sorry it came to this. **Don't leave the room**. Hang in there while the person digests the news. And when they leave, offer your hand—it will help, even if they haven't the heart to take it.

There is no good or happy way to drop this kind of bomb on people. You will carry the bad feeling around with you for a while. But there are better and worse ways to drop it.

The best way is one that is human, constructive, and respectful. The worst way, as in a bad marriage, is to find out things aren't working years into the relationship.

Nine parting shots of managerial wisdom:

1. **Create "stress markers"** for yourself that indicate when you are feeling pushed toward your limits. If you can manage markets and process throughput you can figure out what bugs you—and deal with it.
2. **Take naps**. Or sleep an extra half-hour every night. Those batteries need to recharge.
3. **Hire talented people**. You'll feel less indispensable.
4. **Learn to delegate**. Ditto.
5. **Take frequent short vacations**. Have the family make a list of all the places they want to go—then go there.
6. **Get a hobby**. Your rivals need never know your power secret is scrimshaw.
7. **Walk and think**. Exercise is good for achieving clarity. And it's good, period.
8. **Have a confidant** with whom you can share your thoughts and feelings—not necessarily your spouse.
9. **Slow down**. When you are under stress, you breathe faster and shallower. Inhale. Exhale. Repeat.

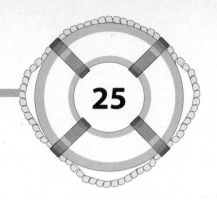

Confession and Conclusion

When we began this book we assured you that it was a book with little ideology or theory. We promised no elegant unifying theme. No grand construct.

The idea was simply to put a practical handbook in your possession to help you through the challenge of your first hundred days as a leader.

Now, standing back from all we have said, we see there is a big idea lurking behind this book. That idea is *balance*. Before we part company, let's talk about balance.

You don't become a leader by being really good at one thing. You can't succeed merely by doing any of the following:

- Meeting quota
- Being shrewd about tactics
- Cutting costs
- Earning the respect of others
- Being a terrific speaker
- Being a skilled motivator

All these things are good, but if you are fantastic at any one
of them but mediocre at all the others, you aren't a good
leader. Because you're out of balance.

What must a leader balance? Practically everything.

A leader balances the *technical* side of the job (the left-hand
column) by knowing the rules, understanding the system,
fulfilling the requirements, achieving the numbers) with the
interpersonal side (the right-hand column) by being able to
elicit the right results from people).

A leader balances short term with long. Financial with non-
monetary values. Doing a few things really well with doing
a lot of things so-so. The needs of one constituency—customers, investors, workers, the industry, the community at
large—with the needs of all the others.

Think of leadership as a see-saw. If one aspect of leading
goes way up, the others go way down. In the old view of things,
that was acceptable and OK. A cost-cutter or turnaround
artist by definition wasn't likely to be a sensitive hand-holder.
The two sets of managerial skills were in tension with one
another. No normal human being was expected to be good
at seemingly opposite skills.

Increasingly, we see that this is a two-dimensional definition
of leadership. A skilled turnaround artist who destroys worker
morale while achieving desired numbers has probably crippled
the company for the long term. The Board has the numbers
they demanded today, but where will they get them tomorrow?

Ends must be balanced with means. It's not enough for
Moses to get his people out of Egypt. He has to get them to

the Promised Land, and still reasonably monotheistic. It's not easy.

The see-saw metaphor still works, but with a twist—that the desired status of the see-saw, over time, is one of balance. Yes, numbers matter. But so do people. A leader who consistently puts numbers over people soon won't have any people with which to achieve any numbers.

It's not that the see-saw is supposed to be paralyzed in perfect homeostasis, with the technical and interpersonal sides permanently eighteen inches off the ground. That kind of artificial and restrictive balance is neither healthy nor practical.

Instead, over time, every aspect of leadership deserves the leader's attention. One end goes up, the other end goes down, but over time, everything is allowed to rise. One end of the see-saw can't triumph at the expense of the other. Both ends get their due.

In this view the leader's primary attribute is not aggression but versatility. It's a profoundly different paradigm from the conventional one. In the conventional paradigm, leaders get by taking. They seize the higher position and keep it. In the altered paradigm, **leaders get by giving.**

Every decision, every conversation, every negotiation moves the fulcrum this way or that way. Even every omission changes the geometry of leveraging.

What we're saying is that nearly everything matters, and that leaders are people who have learned to be thoughtful about everything, without allowing this responsibility to paralyze them.

What else cries out for balance? Your life.

Chances are, the first hundred days won't be days of consummate balance for you and your family, or you and your
own soul.

That's OK in the short run. In the short run, everything is
always out of balance. But as the hundred days stretches into
a year, it is time to pull back a bit and attend to the full spectrum of life's blessings and responsibilities.

Time to pay attention to your health. A great leader who dies
slumped over the desk in the middle of the second quarter
is not much use to the company for the remaining quarters.
For the good of everyone, including yourself, you have to
take care of *you*.

Everyone deserves to get paid. If your spouse or partner holds
you up emotionally for the hundred days, it's payback time
once you find your feet. If you realize you've been neglecting
your kids or friends or parents, take time to poke your head
out of your burrow and reintroduce yourself. If your mind
goes through the workout of a lifetime, make sure you locate
where you left your body—and learn all over again how to
make it work.

They say Bermuda is nice.

**Remember how we started, with the plane in a tailspin,
and you having to land it?**

Tell the truth: that was pretty insane. But here's a better
dream. Four months have passed. Now you're looking back
on your rocky start. You were anxious, and wide-eyed, and

awkward. It's to be expected. No one—except in the movies—steps up to unexpected challenges cool as a summer salad.

You had good days, and you had bad days, but you got through them all.

All in all you did good, and now you get to luxuriate—just a little—in something you didn't have any of a hundred days ago, and now you have maybe a heaping tablespoon of: wisdom.

Being wise means you're no longer a little kid. You know how the system works. You know it can't be done perfectly. But you know it can be done. And you know you can do it.

This is a stunning achievement, and we congratulate you.

Being wise means you understand your own capabilities. It means putting aside most of the reservations you had about being in charge.

If you have taken these instructions to heart, there is one way this wisdom manifests itself so everyone you work with can see. It is that the people who depend on you look at you and say:

"I know what you want."

Isn't that all a leader is, really? Someone that other people can understand. And believe.

Ordinary people, nonleaders, are lucky. They never worry that the eyes of the world are on them. If things on their team or in their department go bad, no one points a finger at them and says, "You. It's your fault everything turned to crap."

Oh, it's nice to not be a leader. You do your work, you punch out, and at night you sleep the sleep of angels.

But for growth, self-fulfillment, and the satisfaction of knowing you made a difference not just for yourself, but for a whole bunch of other people, leading is great too.

And once you are one, it changes you forever.

May you choose well, accidental no longer, and lead.

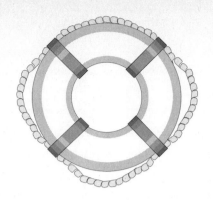

Appendix
Best Books

Some of these are books we consulted during our research. Most, however, are just the strongest titles we are aware of in their topic. We list them in no particular order.

Motivation and Goal Setting: How to Set and Achieve Goals and Inspire Others
by Jim Cairo
Career Press, 1998

Quality Is Free: The Art of Making Quality Certain
by Philip B. Crosby
Mentor Books, 1992

Dr. Deming: The American Who Taught the Japanese About Quality
by Rafael Aguayo
Fireside Books, 1991

Understanding and Changing Your Management Style
by Robert C. Benfari
Jossey-Bass, 1999

Learning to Lead: The Art of Transforming Managers into Leaders
by Jay Alden Conger
Jossey-Bass, 1992

The Dynamics of Taking Charge
John J. Gabarro
Harvard Business School Press, 1987

Leader as Coach: Strategies for Coaching and Developing Others
by David B. Peterson and Mary Dee Hicks
Personnel Decisions International, 1996

The Organized Executive: New Ways to Manage Time, Paper, People and the Electronic Office
by Stephanie Winston
Warner Books, 1994

Communicate With Confidence!
by Dianna Booher
McGraw-Hill, 1994

The New Why Teams Don't Work: What Goes Wrong and How to Make It Right
by Harvey A. Robbins and Michael Finley
Berrett-Koehler, 2000

Guide to Employment Law
by Dana Muir
Jossey-Bass, 2003

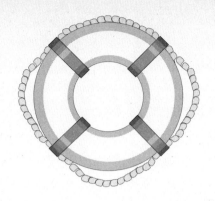

Acknowledgments

We wish to thank Andrea Pedolsky and Nicholas Smith of Altair Literary Agency for their support and good counsel over the years. Also to Susan Williams, Jeff Wyneken, Rob Brandt, Akemi Yamaguchi, Hilary Powers, and the rest of the editorial team at Jossey-Bass, who have impressed us both with their thoroughness and professionalism. Also, special thanks to Nancy Robbins and Jerry de Jaager for their valuable input as this project was just getting started.

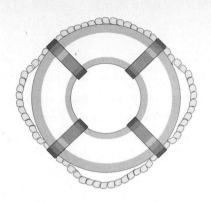

The Authors

Harvey Robbins is a licensed psychologist, business consultant, author, and trainer. For thirty years he has studied the tensions and problems of people in the workplace. His earmarks are humor, a lively presenting style, and a passion for exposing and putting an end to mean-spirited and counterproductive managerial practices. Robbins has consulted with many companies and federal agencies, including ATF, American Express, AlliedSignal, FMC, General Dynamics, AT&T, 3M, Honeywell, IRS, International Multifoods, Johnson & Johnson, Nabisco, Southern Company, Target Stores, Toro, US West, U.S. Customs, and the U.S. Secret Service.

Together with Michael Finley, Robbins won the 1995 Financial Times/Booz-Allen & Hamilton Global Business Award for the Americas for their book *Why Teams Don't Work.* That book, described by many as the "bible of teams," sold over a hundred thousand copies worldwide, was translated into a dozen languages, and has been republished in a revised edition. Robbins also collaborated with Finley on *Why Change Doesn't Work* (Peterson's, 1997) and *Transcompetition* (McGraw-Hill, 1999). *The Accidental Leader* is their fifth book together. Robbins is also author of *Turf Wars* (Scott Foresman, 1989) and *How to Speak and Listen Effectively* (AMACOM, 1991). Since 1982 he has been president of Robbins & Robbins, providing business psychology consulting and training worldwide. Robbins lives with his family in Minnetonka, Minnesota.

Michael Finley brings story-telling, literacy, and a sense of fun that is missing in most business writing to everything he does. He has authored over a dozen books, from his collaborations with Harvey Robbins to his own book *Techno-Crazed* (Peterson's, 1995), charting the dubious progress of computer technology. His work has appeared in *Paris Review, Rolling Stone,* and *Harvard Business Review.* For his essays and columns on change, Finley was designated one of a handful of "Masters of the Wired World" by Financial Times Press of London, in a book by the same name. Others named include Arthur C. Clarke, Nicholas Negroponte, Alvin Toffler, Charles Handy, Al Gore, Tony Blair, and Netscape's Jim Barksdale. In 1985 he won a Pushcart Prize for writing. In 2000, he was named American Reporter Correspondent of the Year. Mike was a regular panelist on the Peabody-nominated program *PBS Mental Engineering,* and he has commented often on the NPR program *Future Tense.* He lives and writes in Saint Paul, Minnesota.

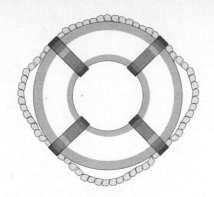

Index

O

Organizations: finding out about leaders of, 54; getting handle on the financials, 55–56; knowing history of your, 53; learning, 90; learning about the failures, 54; responses to poor decision-making, 105–106; understanding competition of your, 53–54; understanding place of your unit in, 54–55; understanding the power relationships in, 56. *See also* Learning environment

Otto, 71–72

Out of the box leadership: importance of, 83–84; seven ways to get out of box, 82; things to check out in your peregrinations, 84–85; transglobal "roaming around," 85

Outside-rule decision-making, 108

P

Parking perks, 113

The Partner leadership style, 34

Partners, 79–80

Patton, G. S., 26

Performing (team stage), 152

Personality types: based delivery of feedback on, 136; creative, 28*e,* 116*e,* 117, 130, 133, 134, 136; doer, 28*e,* 116*e,* 130, 132–133, 136; four distinct, 132; social, 28*e,* 116*e,* 117, 130, 133, 136; thinker, 28*e,* 116*e,* 117, 130, 133, 136

Phil, 63

Picking the low-hanging fruit trick, 63–64

Piotr, 61–63

Planning success: five measures of, 58; importance of, 59–60; paradox of, 60; quick-shot, 60–66

Power: defining decision-making, 97; understanding organizational relationships of, 56. *See also* Empowerment

Predecessors, 102–103

Prioritizing, 65

Q

Quadrants of Success chart, 116*e*

Quick-shot planning: goal stacking trick for, 64–66; learning how to do, 60–61; "little victories" as secret to, 61–63; picking the low-hanging fruit trick for, 63–64

R

Randy, 40

Ray, 115–116

Redefining success, 17–18

Responsibility/emotional response, 3–4

Retooling phase, 15

Riley, 154–155

Roaming around, 83–85

Roanoke naval base supply department, 128–129

S

Satijat, 69

Self-assessment: described, 45; five questions for, 46–48; making a